NEW YORK STATE
GRADE 8
ENGLISH LANGUAGE ARTS TEST

2ND EDITION

NEW YORK STATE GRADE 8
ENGLISH LANGUAGE ARTS TEST
2ND EDITION

Michael Greenberg, M.A.
English Department Head
Great Neck North Middle School

BARRON'S

Acknowledgment: I would like to acknowledge the generous contributions of Professor Gerald Early of Washington University, Assistant Principal Ron Levine, and former 8th graders Ava Hoffman and Cheryl Behnam, both of Great Neck North Middle School, whose written work appears in these pages.

Last, I would like to thank my family members, especially my wife Charlotte, for their invaluable support and encouragement.

All inquiries should be addressed to:
Barron's Educational Series, Inc.
250 Wireless Boulevard
Hauppauge, New York 11788
http://www.barronseduc.com

ISBN-13: 978-0-7641-3359-6
ISBN-10: 0-7641-3359-4
Library of Congress Control Number: 2005938134

PRINTED IN THE UNITED STATES OF AMERICA
9 8 7 6 5 4 3 2

Contents

Preface

In the mid-1990s, the New York State Department of Education published four Learning Standards for English Language Arts:

1. Language for Information and Understanding
2. Language for Literary Response and Expression
3. Language for Critical Analysis and Evaluation
4. Language for Social Interaction

In order to determine whether students were acquiring mastery of these standards, the state created exams that would be administered to students in grades 4, 8, and 11. The grade 8 exam, the subject of this text, was administered for the first time in June 1999. Six years later, in June 2005, the Department of Education revised the format of the exam.

The Grade 8 English Language Arts (ELA) Exam is administered on two consecutive days. The first session includes reading comprehension (multiple choice) and listening-writing; the second session includes only reading-writing. (*Note:* The revised exam eliminated a fourth Composition section.)

One unusual feature of this exam is its interdisciplinary nature. You will notice that the exam tests English language arts skills through social studies or science content, employing material on such diverse topics as cultural differences, immigration, animal life, and the environment.

SCORE REPORTS

Your test will be graded by a group of English teachers. Teachers from other disciplines, such as reading or special education, may also contribute. Different teachers will grade different sections of the exam; possibly, more than one person will score each section.

Score reports are usually printed late in the school year.

Your score report will include several kinds of data. You will notice an overall scaled score, a performance level, and scores for each of the three standards. (The ELA exam does not measure the fourth standard, Language for Social Interaction.)

You probably will be most interested in knowing your overall performance level.

You can think of performance levels this way:

- If you scored a 4 on the exam, your work exceeds standards. You are performing at a consistently high level. A 4 is considered a passing grade.
- If you scored a 3, your work meets the standards. You are on track to take and pass the Grade 11 ELA Regents exam. A 3 is considered a passing grade.
- If you scored a 2, your work approaches the standards. However, a 2 is considered a failing grade. You need some extra help. If you continue to progress, you will take and pass the Grade 11 ELA Regents exam.
- If you scored a 1, your work is considerably below the standards that New York State has set for 8th graders. A 1 is considered a failing grade.

Take a moment to examine the accompanying score report. The first thing you will notice is the vertical bar graph on the left. This student earned a scaled score of 703, which barely earns him a performance level of 3. This is a passing grade. On the lower portion of the report, you will find three horizontal bar graphs in a section called "Referenced Standards." This section lists the student's relative strengths and weaknesses. A glance reveals that his strongest standard is 2, literary response and expression. His scores for standards 1 and 3 are not as strong.

HOW TO USE THIS BOOK

This book is written for 8th graders. You can use it independently or under the supervision of a parent or teacher.

Each chapter includes a ready, set, go format. A test section will be introduced, you will learn the skills needed to master that section, and then you can try out these skills on a sample section. Gradually you will progress toward mastery of all the ELA tasks.

Unless otherwise noted, the reading passages were written by Michael Greenberg.

Chapters 1 through 3 of this book correspond directly to the three sections of the exam. Each can be used to help familiarize you with the format and the content of the exam and, most importantly, assist you in acquiring the skills essential to performing well on the exam. Each chapter provides a rundown of useful strategies and tips, and each concludes with a practice test question.

Each of the four learning standards emphasizes the importance of "the accepted conventions of the English language." This expression refers to conventional standards for spelling, punctuation, capitalization, paragraphing, grammar, and usage. Therefore, Chapter 4 will serve as a handy guide to the English language conventions skills expected of 8th graders.

At the back of the book are two full practice exams. The practice exams are on perforated pages for ease of use. After completing the other sections of the book, you should take these under timed conditions.

The most important factor of all in determining your success on this exam is your own motivation. You *can* improve your reading, listening, and writing skills, but doing so will require sustained effort on your part. In other words, this book will do its part only if you do yours.

English Language Arts (Reading, Writing, and Listening Items)

Performance Levels	Descriptions	Observations
4 SS Range: 739–830	Students consistently show thorough understanding of intermediate-level written and oral text. They can interpret and analyze a variety of texts, use significant literary elements, and synthesize information from related texts to draw conclusions and form insightful opinions, using extensive support. Writing on intermediate-level topics is consistently well organized and thoroughly developed; language is sophisticated and effective, with few or no errors in spelling, grammar, or punctuation.	The height of the graph to the left is an approximate indication of the Scale Score (SS) this student reached in English Language Arts. The performance level indicates this student can perform the majority of what is described for that level as well as what is described for the levels below. The student may also be capable of performing some of the things described in the next higher level, but not enough to have reached that level of performance. Look at the skills and knowledge described in the next higher level. These are the competencies this student needs to demonstrate to show academic growth.
3 SS Range: 701–738 **703**	Students show general understanding somewhat beyond the literal level of intermediate-level written and oral text. They can infer, predict, draw some conclusions, categorize ideas, and make connections between texts, using some relevant support. Writing on intermediate-level topics is generally organized and developed, with appropriate vocabulary, some variety in sentence structure, and some sense of voice; minor errors in spelling, grammar, or punctuation do not interfere with comprehension.	
2 SS Range: 662–700	Students show partial understanding of intermediate-level written and oral text. They can locate information, make basic inferences, use context clues to understand words, and make a few connections between texts, using limited support. Students write on a few familiar topics; writing shows some focus and basic organiztion, using simple sentence structure and vocabulary. Students follow some rules for correct spelling, grammar, and punctuation, but errors sometimes interfere with comprehension.	
1 SS Range: 527–661	Students show minimal understanding of intermediate-level written and oral text. They can locate and recall some details and stated information from the text, attempt to construct short and extended responses, and present some unsupported opinions. Writing consists of brief, general, or repetitive statements and basic vocabulary, and reveals difficulty in organizing thoughts. Errors in spelling, grammar, and punctuation interfere with both readability and comprehension.	

Referenced Standards	SPI	Standards Performance Index (SPI) 20　40　60　80　100	Observations: Standards Performance Index
Standard 1: Student will read, write, listen, and speak for information and understanding.	74		This section of the report presents performance on the Referenced Standards. Each standard is measured by a minimum of 4 items. The Standards Performance Index (SPI) provides an estimate of the number of items that a student could be expected to answer correctly if there had been 100 items for that standard.
Standard 2: Student will read, write, listen, and speak for literary response and expression.	86		The SPI is used to indicate the student's relative strengths and weaknesses in each of the New York State Learning Standards.
Standard 3: Student will read, write, listen, and speak for critical analysis and evaluation.	73		In Standard 1, for example, this student could be expected to respond correctly to 74 out of 100 items.

TIPS FOR TEACHERS

Make no mistake about it: This is a high-stakes exam. Therefore, it is quite possible that school administrators and parents will be very concerned about exam results. What steps can you take—without making yourself and your students completely stressed out—to improve test results?

1. Familiarize yourself with the New York State Department of Education Learning Standards and the content and skills of the Grade 8 ELA exam. It is hoped that your district has been assisting you in this process with a systematic staff development component.
2. Do not fight the standards! After all, what is the state asking here? Only that students should acquire sensible, practical ELA skills by the time they complete the 8th grade. It may not be politically correct to say so, but this is a good exam.
3. Integrate the standards into your instruction. Your literary units should contain ongoing listening, note taking, and writing activities. Students should be reading and writing about more than one source.
4. You cannot overestimate the importance of multiple-choice reading comprehension tasks. Spend time teaching your students how to answer these questions. Design activities that will promote close readings of challenging passages.
5. Stop thinking of yourself as a teacher of fiction. You are a teacher of reading, writing, listening, and, above all, thinking. Vary genres to include nonfiction material such as biographies, newspaper and magazine articles, memoirs, opinion pieces, columns, poetry, and drama.
6. Familiarize your colleagues with the ELA standards and exam. If possible, create interdisciplinary projects that will engage students and satisfy multiple learning objectives. Students who complete a month-long research unit entitled "Immigration and Family Roots" will be preparing for the ELA exam without even realizing it!

7. Make sure your students know that this is a serious exam and that their scores will have real consequences. That said, minimize stress; a pressure-cooker mentality probably will not help anyone come January.

8. Spend some time on test prep activities, using books such as this. Students need to know what to expect in terms of format, skills, and content. However, you would be making a serious error if you teach too much to the test.

TIPS FOR PARENTS

As standards-based education sweeps the nation, schools, parents, and students will learn more and more about new exams. As a parent you can do your part:

1. Learn about the New York State Department of Education Learning Standards, not just in English Language Arts but in all subjects. Your child's school district should be in the process of developing parent education programs. If not, pick up the phone and ask them to.

2. Keep on top of your child's academic work. At the very least, ask to see tests and projects, which will give you a very good sense of the kind of material being taught. Determine whether these assignments are consistent with your sense of current learning standards. Do not be reluctant to discuss this with your child's teachers.

3. Each chapter of this book contains some common-sense tips for parents. You will see that the degree to which you can be helpful will vary, depending upon the task. Obviously, the best you can do is to provide a supportive home environment, one that abets and reinforces your child's academic development.

4. Cooler heads generally prevail. So do not get panicky, and do not communicate your own test anxiety to your child. When test time comes around, you might wish to adjust your family schedule so that your child will be well rested for the exam.

Chapter 1

Reading Comprehension: Part 1 of the Exam

Read. Read books, newspapers, magazines, and brochures. Read fiction and nonfiction; read poetry and prose. Read demanding material; read stuff that is easy. Read at school; read at home; read in the dentist's waiting room. Read for serious purposes, like acquiring information and conducting research. Read also for fun, just because a topic interests you. Read because you have to (school!). Read because you want to.

That is the best strategy for succeeding on reading comprehension tests. However, in this age of convenient, high-tech amusements, quite possibly you have not spent as much time reading as you could have.

Not to worry. If you are a fluent reader, the Reading Comprehension section of the exam can be mastered with just a few commonsense strategies:

- Read the directions that precede each passage. These directions will give you information that will help you understand what you are about to read.
- Initially, read the passage for a general sense of the main idea and organization. Then, as you answer each question, return to the passage as needed in order to find the pertinent details. Do not fret. Do not become frustrated if, after reading the passage just once, you cannot answer a particular question. After all, most readers, as they customarily read, do not try to retain all the details. Simply go back and find what you need. Be aware, too, that certain questions—a small

number—have little or nothing to do with the passage but will test your knowledge of language, not your ability to read.

- Familiarize yourself with the different kinds of graphic organizers you might encounter.
- Remember that multiple-choice questions require you to choose the *best* answer. That means that one or more of the choices may be partially correct. However, you need to choose the one that is completely correct.
- Guess. Your score on this section of the exam is based on the number of questions you answer correctly. Of course, making an intelligent guess is always preferable, that is, choosing between two possible answers. However, you should not leave answers blank, even if it means you are making a wild guess.
- Focus. Sometimes, when you are watching a basketball game, you will hear the announcer proclaim that a certain player is *in the zone*. That means that this particular athlete just cannot miss! He or she seems to be concentrating 100 percent on gaining the upper hand. For the 90 minutes of playing this game, he or she has managed to block out everything else. This kind of mental discipline is an important skill, one that is difficult for some students to acquire, especially if a reading passage is less than fascinating. However, you can acquire it if you find opportunities to practice. Two such opportunities? Class time will afford you many and so will this book.

Actually, the ELA exam has been designed so that two of its three parts test reading comprehension. Part 1 will test your ability to read prose and poetry passages and then answer multiple-choice questions. Part 3, reading-writing, will require you to read and write about two different passages.

In Part 1, you can expect to encounter a wide array of relatively brief reading passages—fiction, nonfiction, poetry, drama, official documents, interviews, sentence completion, and so forth. In addition, you will be asked different types of questions. The purpose of this chapter is to acquaint you with these kinds of questions and to provide you with useful strategies in answering them.

THE TASK

This section of the exam consists of 26 multiple-choice reading comprehension questions. These questions are based on four to six reading selections. You can expect to encounter a wide range of genres. You will come across poetry and prose, fiction and nonfiction. The purposes of these pieces will differ, too. You may find an excerpt from a novel that provides insight into the mind of a character. You may find an article from a magazine that offers information. You may read a poem that wants to amuse or upset you. You may read a myth that offers a life lesson. You may even come across a form to register for some online service. Expect anything.

You will have 45 minutes to complete this section of the exam. Once you are done, you may not return to this section. For most students, time is not a problem.

Your scaled score on the ELA exam consists of the number of points you earn for correct responses. The maximum number of points you can earn—a perfect score—is 39. With that in mind, understand that your score on this section will count for 26 points. That's 26 out of 39, or 66.7 percent. In other words, this is easily the most important section of the exam. Make no mistake about it. If you do poorly on this section, it will be impossible for you to earn a good grade on the exam as a whole.

SHOW YOUR WORK: READING COMPREHENSION

What follows is a strategy certain to improve your performance on multiple-choice reading comprehension tasks.

- Read the piece carefully.
- Read the question. Cover the choices with your hand, and make a "blink" guess. By this, we mean you should write down in your own words what you think the answer might be.
- Begin the process of elimination. Refer to the text. Mark the text if you like. Jot down notes next to each choice.
- Pick the best answer.
- In one or two sentences, explain why your choice is the correct one.

This chapter is going to give you lots of chances to perfect this strategy. As you learn it, you may wonder whether it's practical to devote so much time to one reading comprehension question. The answer is, it probably isn't. By the time you get to the "go" section of this chapter, you will have internalized these procedures. In other words, you'll be doing them in your mind.

GETTING THE MAIN IDEA

As long as you have been reading, teachers and tests have been asking you to cite the main idea of passages, stories, and poems. This exam is no different.

As you read each selection, ask yourself these questions:

- Who or what is the passage about?
- What is the author's purpose in writing the passage?
- Who is the author's audience? To whom is he or she writing?

Take a look at this passage.

It may be difficult for today's youngsters to imagine a time when baseball's World Series was played on crisp early fall afternoons, but for most of the sport's history, that was the case. Of course, the advent of television changed everything. Eventually, baseball adopted an extended play-off formula, and networks televised all games. So the World Series is now played on late October nights, often under near-winter conditions, in order to attract the largest possible prime-time audience.

This was not the case in 1960, when I was a fifth grader in Mrs. Leichter's class.

The 1960 World Series looked like a mismatch. How could anyone think the powerful New York Yankees, winners already of 18 World Series, could lose to the upstart Pittsburgh Pirates? And this was some formidable Yankee team, too, with sluggers like Roger Maris and Mickey Mantle, pitchers Whitey Ford and Luis Arroyo, and superb defenders like third baseman Clete Boyer and second baseman Bobby Richardson. Yet somehow the Pirates had managed to win three of the first six games, all by close scores, while the Yankees in their three victories won by the one-sided scores of 10-0, 12-0, and 16-3.

We could not wait for game 7. Finally, the Yanks would win by another absurd score, once and for all putting an end to the Pirates' unlikely hopes.

Unfortunately, the game was scheduled for a 1:00 start, right smack in the middle of the week. Of course, we all had other plans for that day and time . . . namely, school! Yet Mrs. Leichter, our firm-but-fair teacher, told us she would bring a portable radio to class so that we could listen to the play-by-play.

You could hear a pin drop in room 212 as we listened to every pitch of that seesaw battle. Back and forth went the lead until a

Yankee home run tied the contest. We hoped that the Yanks would prevail before dismissal. However, 3:00 arrived, and we all darted home to our own transistor radios, hoping not to miss too much of the greatest baseball game of our young lives.

I never ran so fast. Since the apartment building where I lived was situated so close to the school, I hardly missed anything. Once home, I gathered my radio and darted down the steps to meet my pal Harry, with whom I had arranged to listen to the game's conclusion.

Alas, fate intervened. In the bottom of the ninth inning, a Pirate second baseman by the name of William Mazeroski drove a pitch over the left-field wall, ending the game, the series, and my dreams. It was another close Pittsburgh victory, this by the score of 10-9, another dagger in the hearts of Yankee fans.

Within a few years, all World Series games were televised. Today, I do not even own a transistor radio.

The author's purpose in writing this passage is (blink guess: _____

_____)

A. to convince major league baseball to schedule World Series day games
B. to compare the strengths and weaknesses of the 1960 World Series contestants
C. to discuss some of the shortcomings of modern technology
D. to recall a memorable event from his childhood

Explain:

O.K., let's apply the Show Your Work strategy to this passage.

■ Read the question and cover the choices. Why did the author write this passage? You should write something that looks like this: "He probably wanted to remember an important event from when he was kid."

■ Now begin the process of elimination. Does the author wish "to convince major league baseball to schedule World Series day games"? The author obviously enjoys reminiscing about this particular day game, and he does say something about unpleasant "near-winter conditions," but it's not really about "convincing." Does the author wish "to compare the strengths and weaknesses of the 1960 World Series contestants"? He does use one paragraph to say that the Series looked like a "mismatch," but that's not his main purpose. Does the author want "to discuss some of the shortcomings of modern technology"? No way. This article isn't at all about modern technology's shortcomings. Does the author wish "to recall a memorable event from his childhood"? The author seems to remember these long-ago events in great detail, and the whole article does seem to recount them, so this seems like the best choice.

Your answer could look like this:

The author's purpose in writing this passage is: (blink guess response:) *He probably wanted to remember an important event from when he was a kid.*

A. to convince major league baseball to schedule World Series Day games—*not really about convincing*
B. to compare the strengths and weaknesses of the 1960 World Series contestants—*yes, but only one paragraph*
C. to discuss some of the shortcoming of modern technology—*no, not at all*
D. to recall a memorable event from his childhood—*yes, in great detail*

Explain:
The whole article goes into a lot of detail about this event from long ago. It obviously affected the author, and now he wants to share it with readers.

And notice how much the final explanation resembles the initial "blink" guess! Did you select **D**? Good start! Now try another.

Just before the presidential election of 1960, Massachusetts Senator John Fitzgerald Kennedy, the Democratic candidate, and Vice President Richard Milhous Nixon, a Republican, squared off in a series of four televised debates. Never before had presidential candidates met in this kind of face-to-face format.

Senator Kennedy was the younger of the two, and many people felt that he lacked the kind of political experience that Nixon had acquired. So for Kennedy, the debates would offer a chance for him to prove he could hold his own on the issues.

Kennedy did indeed hold his own, yet Nixon fared well, too. Many viewers felt that, as far as the issues were concerned, the debates had ended in a draw. However, television, the new medium, simply loved Kennedy. He was handsome and well groomed; he stood casually before the camera, one hand tucked neatly in his pocket, the other gesturing expressively. Now and then, he would flash a radiant smile. He looked relaxed, poised. Nixon, on the other hand, seemed stiff, ill at ease; he had a tendency to fold his arms across his chest in what looked like a defensive posture. Furthermore, Nixon's facial hair grew quickly and dark, and make-up could not conceal his five o'clock shadow.

Kennedy won the election of 1960 by the narrowest of margins. Politicians and voters understood that a new force—television—had entered the political arena.

Use the Show Your Work method to answer this question:

The main idea of the passage is (blink guess: _____

_____)

F. television, the newest medium, played a key role in the election of 1960

G. in the presidential debates of 1960, John Kennedy clearly showed his command of the election's major issues

H. even though Kennedy won the election, the presidential debates probably ended in a tie

J. a candidate's stance on the issues, rather that his personal attractiveness, should be the main factor in an election

Explain:

_____

_____

Your Show Your Work answer might look something like this:

The main idea of the passage is (blink guess: *Kennedy won the election, and TV could have been the difference*)

F. television, the newest medium, played a key role in the election of 1960—*supported by the last paragraph*

G. in the presidential debates of 1960, John Kennedy clearly showed his command of the election's major issues—*true, but no more than Nixon did*

H. even though Kennedy won the election, the presidential debates probably ended in a tie—*true, but not the main idea*

J. a candidate's stance on the issues, rather than his personal attractiveness, should be the main factor in an election—*the passage does not express this opinion*

Explain:

F *is the best answer. Kennedy and Nixon were just about even, but Kennedy looked really good on TV, and Nixon didn't.*

Did you choose **F**? Did your answer resemble this one? Now try one more.

By the time the 1960s drew to a close, Bea Demarco found herself with time on her hands. Unfortunately, her husband, Tony, had died of a heart attack. She realized, too, that her son, Tony, Jr., was fully grown; in fact, he had just started college.

"I always was an idealistic person, living in an idealistic decade," Bea said, "and now the time has come to put my ideals into action."

Bea found herself a job, but it was not just any job. She was going to be working as an assistant teacher in a brand new program for severely developmentally disabled youngsters. These were children who had not previously been in schools. Very few of them could read or write. Some students could not speak. Others could not perform activities of daily living, like dressing themselves or brushing their teeth.

While working with a dedicated group of teachers, therapists, and aides, Bea used behavior modification techniques to teach the children whatever they needed to know in order to function more independently. The job required determination and patience. Bea found that she possessed these traits.

However, she possessed another trait, as well: she was a mother. She knew that sometimes people need a shoulder to lean on, a listener who will not judge harshly. Bea discovered that students, as well as the younger faculty with whom she worked, came to her for these reasons.

People at work needed Bea, as once her husband and son had. Again she felt fulfilled.

This passage is mostly about: (blink guess: _____

_____)

A. how a special education program came into being
B. the challenges of working with students with developmental disabilities
C. the rewards of working as a team
D. how an idealistic person turned her principles into deeds

Explain:

_____

_____

Once again, every answer is at least partially correct. However, the question asks what the passage is "mostly about," and that would be Bea Demarco's transformation from an idealistic person into a person whose deeds speak loudly and clearly. Therefore, the correct choice is **D**.

FINDING THE DETAILS

When you read, you read primarily for ideas, remembering those details that strike you as interesting or unusual. Now and then you hear of a person with a photographic memory, someone who remembers everything he or she reads. However, such people are few and far between.

Most readers need to return to the passage itself in order to locate details. This will be easier for you if you can recall approximately where in the passage the information is located. However, even if you cannot, scanning the passage in order to find the information you need should be easy enough. (The secret lies in looking for key words.)

Be prepared for three different types of recalling-the-details questions:

1. Finding the facts. Authors typically provide facts to support their main ideas.
2. Determining the sequence. In what order do events occur?
3. Cause and effect. Often one event (or characteristic) is responsible for another.

Now read the following passage and use the Show Your Work method to answer the questions that follow.

It is not unusual for pregnant women to suffer from varying degrees of nausea, especially in the first few months of pregnancy. In the late 1950s, chemists in Europe created a new drug—a sleeping pill—that appeared to offer relief from these unpleasant symptoms. The name of this "miracle drug" was thalidomide (*thuh-LID-uh-mide*).

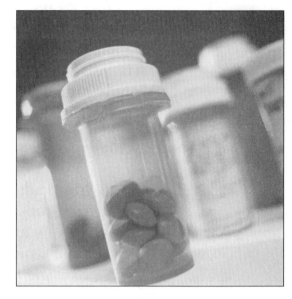

Thalidomide was an over-the-counter drug in Europe. That is, it was available without a prescription.

Over the next few years, however, more than eight thousand deformed babies were born to European women who had taken this drug. Somehow, the drug damaged the skeletal systems of babies, who were born with shortened, malformed arms and legs; some suffered damage to internal organs, as well.

In the early 1960s, the manufacturers of thalidomide wanted to make the drug available to American women, too. However, Dr. Frances Oldham Kelsey, a pharmacologist working for the United States Food and Drug Administration, successfully argued against granting approval for thalidomide distribution. Dr. Kelsey said that drug companies should be required to prove that their products were safe and effective.

In 1962, President John Kennedy gave Dr. Kelsey the Presidential Award for Distinguished Service. Dr. Kelsey's efforts eventually broadened the FDA's powers, resulting in strict regulations in the testing of new drugs in the United States.

---

1. The title of this passage could be: (blink guess _____

_____)

   A. "The Effects of Thalidomide"
   B. "The Unpleasant Side of Pregnancy"
   C. "A Winning Battle Against an Unsafe Drug"
   D. "Europe vs. the United States"

Explain:

_____

_____

2. According to the article, why was the use of thalidomide a problem in Europe but not in the United States? (blink guess: _____

_____)

   F. European women wanted relief from the unpleasant symptoms of pregnancy.
   G. In Europe thalidomide was easily available.
   H. Thalidomide was meant to be used as a sleeping pill.
   J. The use of thalidomide led to birth defects.

Explain:

_____

_____

3. The chart below represents the sequence of events involving thalidomide. Which event belongs in the empty box? (blink guess: _____

_____)

	→ deformed babies born to European women who used thalidomide	→ thalidomide banned in the United States	→ Dr. Kelsey receives Presidential Award for Distinguished Service

A. Thalidomide is made available to European women.
B. Dr. Kelsey investigates early reports on thalidomide.
C. Dr. Kelsey declares that thalidomide is unsafe for pregnant women.
D. The Food and Drug Administration sets tougher standards for testing new drugs.

Explain:

_____

_____

Answers

1. Title questions are just main idea questions packaged differently. The correct answer here is **C**. You might have found **A** ("The Effects of Thalidomide") tempting, but you should be able to determine that this is only partially correct, whereas **C** addresses the entire passage.
2. The use of thalidomide was a problem in Europe and not in the United States because it was an over-the-counter drug and women could obtain it easily. In the United States, Dr. Kelsey addressed that problem. The correct answer is **G**.
3. This question gives you a sequence of four events and asks you determine which one is missing. The correct answer is **A** since only the easy availability of thalidomide could result in birth defects.

Try one more passage.

In 1962, long before most Americans had ever heard the words "environmental protection," Rachel Carson, a prominent marine biologist, published a book called *Silent Spring*. After its publication, Americans would never think of environmental science in quite the same way.

Carson was born in Springdale, Pennsylvania, and graduated from the Pennsylvania College for Women in 1929. Three years later, she earned a master's degree from Johns Hopkins University. For a while, she taught college students. However, for most of her adult life, she worked for the United States Fish and Wildlife Service.

Silent Spring was not Carson's first book. In 1951, she wrote *The Sea Around Us*, in which she introduced her key theme, the interdependence of all living things. She believed that harm done to any single living species would damage the earth's delicate balance and eventually harm other species. According to Carson, human beings were often responsible for tilting the balance.

In *Silent Spring*, Carson identified a particular culprit, DDT, the pesticide that farmers sprayed onto fruits and vegetables. She pointed out that powerful pesticides such as DDT might succeed in killing insects that feed on fruits and vegetables, but they also could poison humans. She cited research that proved that DDT not only stayed in people's systems but that the poison was passed from mother to embryo, so that babies were born with DDT in their systems.

These findings shocked the American public, and before long DDT was banned. Ultimately, Carson's book forced chemical companies to develop less-harmful pesticides and fostered among Americans a sensitivity toward environmental issues.

1. This passage is mostly about (blink guess: _____
   _____)

   A. how a pesticide, DDT, could poison human fetuses
   B. how Rachel Carson's education led to her interest in environmental science
   C. how DDT was banned
   D. how Rachel Carson changed the way Americans think about environmental science

   Explain:

   _____

   _____

2. Which of the following facts was especially useful in proving to the American public the danger of the pesticide DDT? (blink guess: _____
   _____)

   F. DDT could easily destroy insects that prey upon crops.
   G. DDT would remain in people's systems for long periods of time.
   H. DDT would appear in the systems of newborn children.
   J. Treatment of DDT sufferers was extremely costly.

   Explain:

   _____

   _____

3. The passage refers to the earth's "delicate balance." This means that (blink guess: _____

_____)

    A. there exists a relationship among all living things
    B. Carson's fame as a writer and scientist will endure
    C. humans do *not* have to worry about the consequences of their actions
    D. farmers have an especially serious responsibility

Explain: _____

_____

Answers

1. Surely you recognized this as another main idea question. The correct answer is **D**.
2. This detail question requires you to think critically. **G** ("DDT would remain in people's systems for long periods of time") is a strong possibility, but **H** ("DDT would appear in the systems of newborn children") is even stronger. Why? Because, as shocking as **G** might be, **H** is even more upsetting since innocent newborns would suffer from the pesticide. The expression "not only" suggests that **H** was the more upsetting event. Questions like this one should remind you to check out all the options.
3. Return to the passage to locate the key words "delicate balance." Once you have reread that paragraph, you will know that **A** is the only reasonable choice.

MAKING INFERENCES AND DRAWING CONCLUSIONS

The ELA exam will not test only how well you read; it will also test how well you *think* about what you have read. You are going to be asked to use your own judgment, your own ability to think logically about the material in the passage, in order to draw conclusions and make inferences. In this way, you extend the meaning of the text.

Use the Show Your Work method to answer this question, which is based on the Rachel Carson passage that you have just read:

If Rachel Carson were alive today, which of the following might stir her to action? (blink guess: _____

_____)

A. The threat of terrorism as a tool in political negotiations
B. The impact of global warming
C. The escalating price of hardcover books
D. The spread of nuclear weapons among developing nations

Explain:

_____

_____

The correct answer is obviously **B**, because it is the only choice that is clearly an environmental issue. You were able to infer from the Carson passage that since she was a concerned environmentalist, she would probably be concerned today about global warming, a potentially serious environmental issue.

Now reread the thalidomide passage on page 12 and answer the question below.

Which of the following statements is probably true?
F. Prior to the thalidomide scandal, standards for drug testing were not as strict as they are today.
G. Drug companies in Europe do not care about any side effects of the drugs they sell.
H. The American government cares more about its people than do the governments of Europe.
J. All antinausea drugs have dangerous side effects.

Explain:

_____

_____

You can quickly rule out choice **J** since nothing in the passage supports that statement. However, all the others are possibilities, so you really need to look for the best answer. You may find **G** or **H** tempting, but you should be able to sense that they are too general. The essay is not about all drug companies in Europe, nor does it make any large statements about all of the American government. Choice **F** is best because the passage tells you that Dr. Kelsey's actions soon led to tighter legislation; therefore, you can infer that earlier legislation had been less stringent, or strict.

Now read this passage and use the Show Your Work method to answer the questions that follow.

The year 1968 was a troublesome year for the Democratic Party. President Lyndon Johnson, a Democrat elected in 1964, had decided not to run for re-election. President Johnson had inherited a controversial war in Vietnam. The President had suffered unrelenting criticism from war protesters for being unable to resolve the conflict and eventually decided to step aside. The Democratic frontrunner,

Vice President Hubert Humphrey, tried in his campaign to avoid the Vietnam issue. This greatly angered war protesters, who threatened to disrupt the nomination process.

Chicago Mayor Richard Daley, a Democrat, was proud of his city. He was determined to prove to the nation and the world that, despite all the obstacles, the Democratic Convention would be a peaceful, orderly event. There were indeed many obstacles, as Daley saw it. Young protesters came from all over the country; hundreds of thousands filled the city.

Daley responded aggressively. He called out the National Guard, positioned armed police officers all around Chicago's Convention

Hall, and set up barricades with barbed wire. His city now resembled an armed camp.

Even though the vast majority of the demonstrators behaved peacefully, violence soon erupted with a fury. To the millions of Americans watching on television, it seemed the fault of the police, not the protesters. Images of Daley's helmeted police officers clubbing and beating young men and women and dragging them, bleeding, into police vans found their way into America's living rooms. The National Guard, wearing masks, hurled tear gas canisters. Protesters, sitting peacefully on the ground, were beaten into submission. Nightstick-wielding police relentlessly pursued escaping protesters, who begged in vain for help.

Inside the Convention Hall, Democratic political leaders became aware of the riots just outside. Connecticut's Senator Abraham Ribicoff condemned Daley for his "Gestapo[1] tactics."

More than seven hundred civilians suffered injuries; more than six hundred were jailed. Even the news reporters, trying to cover the event, were not immune to the charging "peace" officers.

The New York Times also placed the blame squarely onto Daley's shoulders. According to the *Times*, peaceful protestors had not been permitted to assemble. Even worse, police violence had denied them the opportunity to protest against the war in Vietnam and a Democratic Party that seemed unresponsive to their concerns.

Just months later, Richard Nixon would soundly defeat Humphrey in the election of 1968.

---

[1]**Gestapo:** armed Nazi officers

1. The purpose of this passage is to (blink guess: _____
   _____)
   A. discuss the political issues facing the Democratic
      Party in 1968
   B. explain the reasons for protest in 1968
   C. explain why Hubert Humphrey failed to defeat
      Richard Nixon in the 1968 presidential election
   D. explain the events that led to the Chicago riots of
      1968

   Explain:

   _____

   _____

2. Which of the following statements is probably true?
   F. All of the Chicago protesters behaved peacefully.
   G. The Vietnam issue contributed to the defeat of the
      Democrats in the 1968 presidential election.
   H. The events in Chicago ended the protest movement,
      once and for all.
   J. The events in Chicago enhanced Richard Daley's
      standing in the Democratic Party.

   Explain:

   _____

   _____

3. By the time the Chicago Convention ended, most neutral observers had probably learned that (blink guess:

_____

_____)

  A. peaceful protests do not always end peacefully

  B. the Democratic Party was eager to address the concerns of the antiwar protesters

  C. Mayor Richard Daley did not care about his city's image

  D. news reporters covering violent events did not need to worry about their own safety

Explain:

_____

_____

4. What would be a good title for this article? (blink guess: _____

_____)

  F. "A Bad Year for the Democrats"

  G. "Nixon Defeats Humphrey in 1968"

  H. "Protests and Violence Spoil Democratic Convention"

  J. "National Guard Gets Too Aggressive"

Explain:

_____

_____

Answers

1. Once again, a main idea question. You could argue that **A, B,** and **C** are all partially true, but **D** is the most comprehensive reply.

2. Here you are being asked to extend the meaning of the text. None of these questions is addressed explicitly in the passage, yet you must apply your own logic to the events discussed therein. You can immediately rule out

F, since the passage says that the "vast majority," but not all, were nonviolent. Common sense should tell you that the riots in Chicago did not end the protest movement nor would they have enhanced Daley's status among Democrats (the passage tells you that Senator Ribicoff, for one, publicly condemned Daley's actions). The best answer is **G**, since the Democrats' failure to address the Vietnam issue led not only to the events in Chicago but can easily be connected to the election results.

3. Here is another drawing conclusions-type question. You must pay attention to the phrase "neutral observers" since protesters, on the one hand, or the National Guard, on the other, would probably have very biased views. You might find **C** tempting, because, in the final analysis, Daley's actions harmed his city's image. Yet the passage clearly tells you that Daley's errors were probably the result of his caring too much about his city's image as a peaceful, orderly place. The best answer is **A**.

4. Expect to come across a question that asks you for a title. It's certainly a main idea question, but it also requires you to draw a conclusion about what's most important in the story. Choice **F** is too general, and choices **G** and **J** are too specific. **H**, the correct choice, most clearly and comprehensively expresses the content of the article.

When you infer, you examine the evidence and reach an understanding. One particular inference the ELA exam will ask you to make is to differentiate between fact and opinion. Consider the following advertisement:

Bernard's Chocolate Shop first opened its doors in 1916, when Herbert Bernard emigrated from Paris to these shores. For several years, the shop failed to realize a profit. However, Herbert was confident about the quality of his product, so every day, for an hour, he stood on the corner of Grand and Sussex Streets, distributing free samples to passersby. Gradually business improved. Today, under the stewardship of Herbert's grandchildren, the Bernard Chocolate Emporium ships boxes of the world's finest chocolate to America's top stores and restaurants and to 57 countries around the world.

1. Which of the following excerpts expresses an opinion? (blink guess:_____

_____)

   A. "Bernard's Chocolate Shop first opened its doors in 1916"

   B. "For several years, the shop failed to realize a profit"

   C. "he stood on the corner of Grand and Sussex Streets, distributing free samples to passersby"

   D. "the Bernard Chocolate Emporium ships boxes of the world's finest chocolate"

Explain:

_____

_____

You probably realized that answers **A**, **B**, and **C** are expressions of fact. **D** expresses an opinion. The company would like you to believe that its chocolates are "the world's finest," but until you've swallowed a few, that's just a lot of talk.

Try this one on your own:

> Here it is, the game you've been waiting for: Lunar Labyrinth. Gekko's research and development boys have been working on this one for two years, and now it's yours for $89.99. The price may be high, but this is money you won't mind spending. You've never seen graphics like these. And when you meet the Moon Minotaur, you'll forget all previous definitions of danger. Say goodbye to TV, to family and friends, to meals and exercise. Once you get your hands on Lunar Labyrinth, you'll be hanging out on the moon.

1. Which of these excerpts is an expression of fact? (blink guess:_____

_____)

   A. "Here it is, the game you've been waiting for"
   B. "now it's yours for $89.99"
   C. "You've never seen graphics like these"
   D. "And when you meet the Moon Minotaur, you'll forget all previous definitions of danger"

Explain:

_____

_____

Advertising has two purposes: to inform and to appeal to your emotions. As you examined the choices, you probably noticed that only **B** provides factual information: This excerpt gives you the price, nothing more.

A SPECIAL CASE: LITERATURE

Undoubtedly you are already familiar with literary terms and techniques. That is to your advantage, because you will probably see some questions about them on Part 1 of the ELA exam.

Here are some terms you should know:

- *Mood* is the atmosphere and feeling a writer creates in a work through the choice of setting, details, descriptions, and events.
- *Figurative language* is language that represents one concept with another. A *metaphor* is one type. "Life's but a walking shadow, a poor player/ That struts and frets his hour upon the stage." In this excerpt from *Macbeth*, Shakespeare compares life to a shadow and an actor ("player"). A *simile* also compares two unlike things but uses "as" or "like." "My heart is like a soaring bird" is an example of a simile. Figurative language abounds in our everyday speech. We say that a smooth speaker has a "honeyed tongue" or that someone who has failed in an endeavor has "struck out." Be sensitive to these as you hear them. (You may even hit a grand slam on the ELA exam!)
- *Personification* is a figure of speech in which human characteristics are given to nonhuman things. "Winter whispered its arrival in my ear." Here, "winter" is personified (a season cannot whisper; only humans can).
- *Imagery* is the use of concrete details that appeal to the five senses. "The rotting stink of summer's uncollected refuse" may well suggest some unpleasant images.
- *Setting* is the time and place in which a story or poem takes place. For example, Harper Lee's novel *To Kill a Mockingbird* is set in the deep South around the middle of the twentieth century. Setting matters a great deal in this novel because, as that time and place suggest, racism plays a major role.
- *Point of view* refers to the way a story is told (the *narrator* refers, of course, to the teller of that story). The most common forms of narration are *first person*, in which the narrator is a character in the story, and *third person*, in which the narrator is not a character in the story. Note the difference:

As I placed the carefully wrapped package onto the park bench, I looked up and saw Molly walking across the street. I hoped she had not seen me. (first person)

George, anxiously hoping no one was watching him, placed a carefully wrapped package onto the bench. However, Molly saw him and could not help thinking he was acting strangely. (third person)

- *Plot* refers to the events that comprise the story; in other words, the plot is what happens. The plot consists of three elements. The first is *conflict*, the struggle between two opposing forces. The second is the *climax* (sometimes called the *crisis*), the point at which the main character acts to resolve the conflict. The third is *resolution*, or the consequences of the climax. If you are familiar with W. W. Jacobs's famous story "The Monkey's Paw," you are probably aware of the way the conflict changes as the story progresses. Ultimately, so-and-so must use the third wish in order to undo the results of the previous two; this moment is the story's crisis.

- *Theme* is the author's message, or the point of the piece. What is the theme of "The Monkey's Paw"? You could argue that the author was saying that you should be happy with what you have. You might say the theme is that everything comes with a price. (Be careful about confusing *plot* and *theme*. Remember that the plot is what happens in the story, and that the theme is the point of the story.)

- *Irony* is the difference between the reader's expectation and the actual event in a story. The ending of Guy de Maupassant's story "The Necklace" is ironic because Mathilde Loisel, the main character, sacrificed a great deal to pay for a diamond necklace that was not authentic.

- *Rhyme scheme* refers, of course, to a pattern of end rhyme, the use of the same sounds at the end of lines of poetry. In determining rhyme scheme, you simply assign the same letter, starting with "a," to lines ending with the same sound. Consider the following example from Robert Herrick's "Upon Julia's Clothes":

> Whenas in silks my Julia goes,
> Then, then (methinks) how sweetly flows
> That liquefaction of her clothes.

You would begin by assigning the letter "a" to the first line, which ends with "goes." You will notice immediately that the second and third lines, ending respectively with "flows" and "clothes," end with just about the same sound. Therefore, the rhyme scheme of the stanza is aaa.

Now take a look at a few lines from Andrew Marvell's "To His Coy Mistress":

> Had we but world enough, and time,
> This coyness, lady, were no crime.
> We would sit down, and think which way
> To walk, and pass our long love's day.

Can you figure out the rhyme scheme? (It is aabb. The first and second lines rhyme, and so do the third and fourth.)

■ *Alliteration* is the repetition of initial consonant sounds in neighboring words. This definition is itself alliterative: similar successive sounds.

Now read this poem and see how well you can answer the questions that follow.

The Eagle
By Alfred Lord Tennyson

> He clasps the crag[1] with crooked hands,
> Close to the sun in lonely lands,
> Ring'd with the azure[2] world, he stands.
>
> The wrinkled sea beneath him crawls,
> He watches from his mountain walls,
> And like a thunderbolt he falls.

[1]**crag:** a steep hill or cliff
[2]**azure:** sky blue

1. The expression "with crooked hands" is an example of (blink guess: _____

   _____)

   A. personification
   B. simile
   C. setting
   D. none of the above

   Explain:

   _____

   _____

2. The first stanza's rhyme scheme is (blink guess: _____

   _____)

   F. aba
   G. abb
   H. aaa
   J. aab

   Explain:

   _____

   _____

3. The mood of the poem can best be described as (blink guess: _____

   _____)

   A. joyful
   B. uneasy
   C. satisfied
   D. comic

   Explain:

   _____

   _____

4. Which line contains the best example of alliteration?
   F. line 1
   G. line 3
   H. line 4
   J. line 6

   Explain:

   _____

   _____

Answers

1. Eagles do not have hands; they have claws. Therefore the correct answer is **A**, personification.
2. Since all three lines end with the same sounds, the answer is **H** (aaa).
3. Even if you do not know that "uneasy," choice **B**, means "nervous," "unsettled," or "on edge," you should be able to use the process of elimination to come up with this correct answer since clearly the poem's mood is not "joyful," "satisfied," or "comic." In this poem, an eagle stands on the edge of a cliff, isolated, regal, until suddenly in the last line he spots his prey and falls upon it "like a thunderbolt." The first five lines create this unease, this tension, with the harsh sounds of the first line, the heat of the sun, the loneliness of the eagle's perch, and the absence of any action. The last line, suggesting the sudden destruction of his prey, adds to it in another way.
4. Can you hear the repetition of a hard "c" sound in line 1? Three words—"clasps," "crag," and "crooked"—all begin with that sound. Therefore, **F** is the correct choice.

Emily Dickinson is one of America's most beloved poets. Sometimes her poems can be rather tricky, but this one is fairly straightforward:

He Ate and Drank the Precious Words
By Emily Dickinson

He ate and drank the precious words.
His spirit grew robust[1];
He knew no more that he was poor,
Nor that his frame was dust.
He danced along the dingy days,
And his bequest[2] of wings
Was but a book. What liberty
A loosened spirit brings!

1. This poem is mostly about (blink guess: _____
   _____)

   A. a man with a drinking problem
   B. the joys of living in a democracy
   C. the relationship between a father and his heirs
   D. a man who loved literature

   Explain:

   _____

   _____

2. The rhyme scheme of this poem's first four lines is (blink guess: _____
   _____)

   F. abcb
   G. abab
   H. aaba
   J. aabc

   Explain:

   _____

   _____

[1]**robust:** healthy, sturdy
[2]**bequest:** a gift to a descendant

3. The metaphor in lines 6 and 7 compares a book to (blink guess: _____

_____)

  A. dust
  B. wings
  C. precious words
  D. music

Explain:

_____

_____

Answers

1. There is no getting away from these main idea questions! Even the poem's title should tell you that it is about a man who lives through the power of language. The correct answer is **D**.

2. The second and fourth lines rhyme ("robust" and "dust"); the first and third do not. Therefore, the correct answer is abcb (**F**).

3. The power of a book enables the man to rise—to fly—above his poverty, to "dance along the dingy days." This metaphor reinforces the poem's theme, the power of literature to change a person's life completely. The correct answer is **B**. (Do not be fooled by choice **C**, "precious words." A book may consist of precious words, but it is not being compared to them.)

This next passage is from Charles Dickens's novel, *Great Expectations*. In it, the narrator, Pip, recalls a highly memorable first meeting. (Note the vocabulary words below the passage.)

In an arm-chair, with an elbow resting on the table and her head leaning on that hand, sat the strangest lady I have ever seen, or shall ever see.

She was dressed in rich materials—satins, and lace, and silks—all of white. Her shoes were white. And she had a long white veil dependent from her hair, and she had bridal flowers in her hair, but her hair was white. Some bright jewels lay sparkling on the table. Dresses less splendid than the dress she wore, and half-packed trunks, were scattered about. She had not quite finished dressing, for she had but one shoe on—the other was on the table near her hand—her veil was but half arranged, her watch and chain were not put on, and some lace for her bosom lay with those trinkets, and with her handkerchief, and gloves, and some flowers, and a prayer-book, all confusedly heaped about the looking-glass.[1]

It was not in the first few moments that I saw all these things, though I saw more of them in the first moments than might be supposed. But, I saw that everything within my view which ought to be white, had been white long ago, and had lost its lustre,[2] and was faded and yellow. I saw that the bride within the bridal dress had withered like the dress, and like the flowers, and had no brightness left but the brightness of her sunken eyes. I saw that the dress had been put upon the rounded figure of a young woman, and that the figure upon which it now hung loose had shrunk to skin and bone. Once, I had been taken to see some ghastly waxwork at the fair, representing I know not what impossible personage lying in state.[3] Once, I had been taken to one of our old marsh churches to see a skeleton in the ashes of a rich dress that had been dug out of a vault under the church pavement. Now, waxwork and skeleton seemed to have dark eyes that moved and looked at me. I should have cried out, if I could.

---

[1]**looking-glass:** mirror
[2]**lustre:** shine

1. In this passage, the narrator notes the contrast between (blink guess: _____

   _____)

   A. his own age and the age of the woman he has met
   B. the luxury of this setting and the poverty he is accustomed to
   C. his own mood and the mood of the woman he has just met
   D. the color that things should be and the color that they actually are

   Explain:

   _____

   _____

2. Which of the following best describes the narrator's reaction to what he has just seen? (blink guess: _____

   _____)

   F. fear and amazement
   G. curiosity and amusement
   H. anger and bitterness
   J. gratitude and relief

   Explain:

   _____

   _____

3. "It was not in the first few moments that I saw all these things, though I saw more of them in the first moments than might be supposed." This excerpt describes the narrator's (blink guess: _____

   _____)

   A. concern
   B. alertness
   C. shyness
   D. poverty

   Explain:

   _____

   _____

[3]**lying in state:** being displayed to the public prior to burial

Answers

1. This is a tough question, but the answer can be found in the next-to-last paragraph: "I saw that everything within my view which ought to be white, had been white long ago, and had lost its lustre, and was faded and yellow." These lines, as well as those that follow, show that the correct answer is **D**.

2. The beginning of the passage suggests strangeness and amazement, and the end ("I should have cried out") fear, so the best answer is **F**.

3. The narrator indicates that he observed in the first moments of this meeting much more he would have thought possible. Therefore, you can conclude that he is an alert and perceptive narrator; the answer is **B**.

WORDS IN CONTEXT

You can certainly count on seeing a few questions of this kind, in which you will be asked to figure out the meaning of a word you might not know. If you are lucky, you may already know the meaning of the word. In that case, all you will need to do is determine if that meaning fits the context of the sentence. That is important, because words have many meanings, and you will want to choose one that fits the context.

If you do not know the meaning of the word, you can rely on two strategies. The first is to try to replace the unknown word with one that makes sense to you.

Consider this example:

When Mary found herself in this latest *quagmire*, she knew she would have to overcome the temptation to panic.

The word *quagmire* probably means (blink guess: _____

_____)

A. difficulty
B. building
C. edition
D. fashion

Explain:

_____

_____

The overall sense of the passage tells you that Mary is in a difficult situation, so much so that she must try hard not to panic. Therefore, you would choose **A**.

Sometimes, the sentence will not point clearly to the word's meaning. In that case, you must examine surrounding sentences in order to gain a sense of the passage's dominant mood and meaning. Try this one.

When it came to painting, Phillip was a mere *dilettante*. Yes, he enjoyed visiting the Metropolitan Museum of Art, and, on occasion, when he found a class hopelessly boring, he would try his hand at sketching a profile of the lecturer. However, he could not distinguish a Rembrandt from a Breughel, nor a Renoir from a Degas.

The word *dilettante* probably means (blink guess: _____

_____)

F. expert
G. collector
H. amateur
J. professor

Explain:

_____

_____

In the first sentence, the word "mere" suggests a certain insufficiency, but its presence alone is probably not enough to give you the correct answer. However, as you read the remainder of the passage, you will note that Phillip's appreciation of painting is superficial, at best, since he cannot distinguish the work of one painter from another's. The only possible answer then is **H**.

Now try these few on your own.

James Meredith had served in the United States Air Force. However, if he believed that his military service made him equal in the eyes of all Mississippians, he was mistaken. James Meredith was an African-American. As a result, three times the University of Mississippi forcibly denied him an opportunity to enroll in classes. Finally, in 1962, under the auspices of Justice Department officers, Meredith began his college education.

1. The word *auspices* probably means (blink guess: _____ _____)

   A. prejudice
   B. protection
   C. advice
   D. weapons

Explain:

_____

In 1964, Dr. Martin Luther King, Jr., was awarded the Nobel Peace Prize. King, like his predecessor Mahatma Gandhi, believed in passive resistance. King felt that the only way to address unjust laws and regulations was to break those laws nonviolently, accept the consequences for doing so, and in the process bring to the public's attention the fact that those laws and regulations were indeed unjust.

2. The word *passive* probably means (blink guess: _____

_____)

F. nonaggressive

G. sneaky

H. lengthy

J. intentional

Explain:

_____

_____

At the same time that many African-American leaders were hoping to live peacefully alongside white Americans, Malcolm X became the most outspoken advocate of black power and separatism. While Malcolm believed in the brotherhood of men, he also felt that white Americans would never embrace African-Americans as equals. He said that African-Americans should fight for their rights "by any means necessary."

3. The word *advocate* probably means (blink guess: ____

_____)

A. opponent

B. worker

C. voter

D. supporter

Explain:

_____

_____

Answers

1. **B** ("protection") is the best choice. Since the University of Mississippi "forcibly" prevented him from enrolling, Meredith would require protection.

2. The passage establishes King's belief that while it was necessary to oppose unjust policies, this opposition had to be nonviolent. Therefore, **F** ("nonaggressive") is correct.

3. The very first sentence contrasts Malcolm's beliefs with those who believed that whites and blacks could live peacefully side by side. He became a spokesperson for, or supporter of, separatism. The correct answer is **D**.

A SAMPLE READING COMPREHENSION SECTION

This next section will give you a chance to practice your reading comprehension skills. The passages are similar to those you will find on the ELA exam. Give yourself no more than 45 minutes to complete this activity. Because of the time limit, you will probably not be able to show in writing all of the Show Your Work strategies you learned and used in this chapter. (In fact, the sample test section does not call for them.) However, that doesn't mean you can't use them mentally. Make a blink guess, return to the passage to select a correct response, and explain in your mind why that it is the best answer.

DIRECTIONS

In wartime, soldiers often write home to their families and friends. Sullivan Ballou, a Union soldier, wrote this letter to his wife just a week before he was killed in the Battle of Bull Run. Read the letter carefully, and answer the questions that follow.

July the 14th, 1861
Washington, D.C.

My very dear Sarah:

The indications are very strong that we shall move in a few days—perhaps tomorrow. Lest I should not be able to write to you again, I feel impelled to write lines that may fall under your eye when I shall be no more.

Our movement may be one of a few days duration and full of pleasure—and it may be one of severe conflict and death to me. Not my will, but thine O God, be done. If it is necessary that I should fall on the battlefield for my country, I am ready. I have no misgivings about, or lack of confidence in, the cause in which I am engaged, and my courage does not halt or falter. I know how strongly American Civilization now leans upon the triumph of the Government, and how great a debt we owe to those who went before us through the blood and suffering of the Revolution. And I am willing—perfectly willing—to lay down all my joys in this life, to help maintain this government, and to pay that debt.

But, my dear wife, when I know that with my own joys I lay down nearly all of yours, and replace them in this life with cares and sorrows—when, after having eaten for long years the bitter fruit of orphanage myself, I must offer it as their only sustenance to my dear little children—is it weak or dishonorable, while the banner of my purpose floats calmly and proudly in the breeze, that my unbounded love for you, my darling wife and children, should struggle in fierce, though useless, contest with my love of country?

I cannot describe to you my feelings on this calm summer night, when two thousand men are sleeping around me, many of them enjoying the last, perhaps, before that of death—and I, suspicious that Death is creeping behind me with his fatal dart, am communing with God, my country, and thee.

Sarah, my love for you is deathless, it seems to bind me to you with mighty cables that nothing but Omnipotence could break; and yet my love of Country comes over me like a strong wind and bears me irresistibly on with all these chains to the battlefield.

The memories of the blissful moments I have spent with you come creeping over me, and I feel most gratified to God and to you that I have enjoyed them so long. And hard it is for me to give them up and burn to ashes the hopes of future years, when God willing, we might still have lived and loved together and seen our sons grow up to honorable manhood around us. Something whispers to me that I shall return to my loved ones unharmed. If I do not, my dear Sarah, never forget how much I love you, and when my last breath escapes me on the battlefield, it will whisper your name.

As for my little boys, they will grow as I have done, and never know a father's love and care. Little Willie is too young to remember me long, and my blue-eyed Edgar will keep my frolics with him among the dimmest memories of his childhood. Sarah, I have unlimited confidence in your maternal care and your development of their characters.

Sullivan

1. What is the struggle that the author addresses in his letter?
   A. He questions his religious faith.
   B. He questions whether he is fighting for a worthwhile cause.
   C. His love of his country conflicts with his love of his family.
   D. He is uncertain about his own courage in facing life-and-death situations on the battlefield.

2. Which of the following is an example of personification?

   F. "Death is creeping behind me with his fatal dart"
   G. "Our movement may be one of a few days duration and full of pleasure"
   H. "When my last breath escapes me on the battlefield"
   J. "I am willing—perfectly willing—to lay down all my joys in this life"

3. In the second paragraph, the author describes a debt he feels to

   A. the men who serve under him
   B. his own commanding officer
   C. Americans of an earlier generation who fought for independence
   D. his wife and sons

4. The author says that he has "eaten for long years the bitter fruit of orphanage myself." This statement probably explains why

   F. he fears leaving his own boys without a father
   G. he has great confidence in his wife's ability to raise their children on her own
   H. he still hopes he may return to his family unharmed
   J. he brings to the battlefield so many wonderful memories of his family

5. "Lest I should not be able to write to you again, I feel impelled to write lines that may fall under your eye when I shall be no more." Which of these words probably means about the same as *impelled*?

   A. embarrassed
   B. overjoyed
   C. tearful
   D. driven

6. How does the author contrast his situation with that of the other soldiers awaiting the call to battle?

   F. Most of the other soldiers do not have wives and children.

   G. Most of the other soldiers sleep peacefully, while the author cannot.

   H. Most of the other soldiers are unaware of the historical significance of the war.

   J. Most of the other soldiers are confident of the battle's outcome.

DIRECTIONS

The poem you are about to read describes a situation painfully familiar to Civil War mothers on both sides: a son going off to enlist. Read the poem, and then answer the questions that follow.

Enlisted Today
Author unknown

I know the sun shines, and the lilacs are blowing,
And summer sends kisses by beautiful May—
Oh! to see all the treasures the spring is bestowing,
And think my boy Willie enlisted today,

It seems but a day since at twilight, low humming,
I rocked him to sleep with his cheek upon mine,
While Robby, the four-year old, watched for the coming
Of father, adown the street's indistinct line.

It is many a year since my Harry departed,
To come back no more in the twilight or dawn:
And Robby grew weary of watching, and started
Alone on the journey his father had gone.

It is many a year—and this afternoon sitting
At Robby's old window, I heard the band play,

And suddenly ceased dreaming over my knitting,
To recollect Willie is twenty today.

And that, standing beside him this soft May-day
morning,
And the sun making fold of his wreathed cigar smoke,
I saw in his sweet eyes and lips a faint warning,
And choked down the tears when he eagerly spoke:

"Dear mother, you know how these Northmen
are crowing,
They would trample the rights of the South in the dust,
The boys are all fire; and they wish I were going—"
He stopped, but his eyes said, "Oh, say if I must!"

I smiled on the boy, though my heart it seemed breaking,
My eyes filled with tears, so I turned them away,
And answered him, "Willie, 'tis well you are waking—
Go, act as your father would bid you, today!"

I sit in the window, and see the flags flying,
And drearily list to the roll of the drum,
And smother the pain in my heart that is lying
And bid all the fears in my bosom be dumb.

I shall sit in the window when summer is lying
Out over the fields, and the honey-bee's hum
Lulls the rose at the porch from her tremulous
sighing,
And watch for the face of my darling to come.

And if he should fall—his young life he has given
For freedom's sweet-sake; and for me, I will pray
Once more with my Harry and Robby in Heaven
To meet the dear boy that enlisted today.

7. The poem's rhyme scheme is
   A. aabb
   B. abcb
   C. aaba
   D. abab

8. "I . . . bid all the fears in my bosom be dumb." In this case, the word *dumb* probably means
   F. ignorant
   G. soft-spoken
   H. incapable of speaking
   J. attentive

9. The mood of this poem can best be described as
   A. frantic
   B. reflective
   C. patriotic
   D. cheerful

10. The first stanza establishes
   F. a contrast between a joyful time of year and Willie's decision to enlist
   G. the fact that Willie will fight for the South
   H. that Willie is the mother's youngest child
   J. that the mother's husband, Harry, left home long ago

11. These lines appear in the sixth stanza:

"The boys are all fire; and they wish I were going—"
He stopped, but his eyes said, "Oh, say if I must!"

The poet includes these lines to show that
   A. Willie believes deeply in the Southern cause
   B. many of Willie's friends are eager to fight in the war
   C. Willie is not sure if enlisting is the right thing to do
   D. Willie's father surely would have approved of his decision

DIRECTIONS

All wars, including the Civil War, produce their share of records and documents. Read the following document, and answer the questions below.

CERTIFICATE

TO BE GIVEN TO VOLUNTEERS AT THE TIME OF THEIR DISCHARGE TO ENABLE THEM TO RECEIVE THEIR PAY, ETC.

I certify on honor that Jacob Kleinman, a second class Musician of Band of Third Regiment of Infty PRVC, Volunteers of the State of Pennsylvania, born in Germany, age 41 years, 5 feet 7 inches high, dark complexion, blue eyes, grey hair and by occupation a Musician, having joined the Band on its original organization at Camp Trunally, D.C., and enrolled in it at the Muster into the Service of the United States at Camp Trunally, D.C. on the seventeeth day of September, 1861 for the term of three years and having entitled to pay and subsistence for traveling to place of enrollment and whatever other allowances are authorized to Volunteer soldiers, and militia, so discharged. He has received fifty-five dollars and three cents advanced by the United States on account of clothing given in duplicate at Harrison Landing, Virginia, this Seventh day of August 1862.

H. G. Sickel
Col. Commanding Regmt.

12. How long did Jacob Kleinman serve the third regiment?

   F. approximately five years

   G. three weeks

   H. a little less than one year

   J. a little more than one year

13. The document contains a detailed physical description of Jacob Kleinman. This information is included because

   A. the Army wanted to be sure the correct person was paid

   B. the Army suspected Kleinman of various criminal offenses

   C. many soldiers resembled Kleinman physically

   D. Kleinman was too old to continue serving in the Army

14. The document claims that Kleinman was "entitled to pay and subsistence for traveling to place of enrollment and whatever other allowances are authorized." In this case, the word *subsistence* probably means

   F. reward

   G. means of support

   H. penalty

   J. uniform

DIRECTIONS

Here is a document—actually a poster—of a very different nature. Read it carefully, and answer the questions that follow.

$20 REWARD.

Ranaway from the Subscriber, on the 22nd December last, his negro man MAR-TIN, aged about 23 years. He has a pleasing countenance, round face, is quick spoken, and can tell a very plausible story; he is a shining black, stout built, with large limbs, short fingers, and small feet; the toe next to his great toe has been mashed off.

The above reward will be paid on his delivery to me, or at any Jail in North Carolina.

JAMES R. WOOD.

Wadesboro, Feb. 5, 1844.

15. The poster says that Martin "can tell a very plausible story." In this case, *plausible* probably means
   A. incredible
   B. detailed
   C. descriptive
   D. believable

16. The poster offers several detailed descriptions of Martin's physical appearance. Which of the following would have been most distinctive?

F. "A pleasing countenance, round face"
G. "Stout built, with large limbs"
H. "Shining black"
J. "The toe next to his great toe has been mashed off"

17. In all likelihood, this poster would have appeared in

A. Pennsylvania
B. North Carolina
C. Texas
D. Maine

DIRECTIONS

Read BOTH the introductory material and the poem that follows. William Comfort was a prisoner at Andersonville when he wrote this poem in 1863. Then answer the questions.

In Andersonville, Georgia, in the midst of a raging Civil War, the South established Andersonville Prison. The prison was designed to hold no more than 10,000 Northern prisoners, yet at one time as many as 33,000 were confined there. Conditions were horrifying, and, as a result, over one 13-month period, 13,700 men died. One of the causes of the overcrowding was political; the leaders of the North and South could not agree upon a prisoner exchange arrangement, and so prisoners at Andersonville and elsewhere languished amid horrible conditions. Later, when the North invaded Georgia and captured the prison, a United States military court convicted the prison superintendent, Captain Henry Wirz, of murder. He was hanged in 1865.

A Cry from Andersonville Prison
By William Comfort

When our country called for men, we came from forge
and hill,
From workshop, farm and factory the broken ranks to fill.
We left our quiet happy home and those we loved so well,
To vanquish all our Union's foes or fall where others fell.
But now in prison drear we languish and 'tis our
constant cry,
Oh, ye who yet can save us . . . will you leave us here
to die?

Did the voice of slander tell ye that our hearts were weak
with fear?
That all, or nearly all, of us were captured in the rear?
But the scars upon our bodies from the musket ball
and shell,
The missing legs and shattered arms a truer tale will tell;
We have tried to do our duty in the sight of God on high,
And ye who can yet save us now leave us here to die.

There are hearts with hope still beating in our
"Northern Homes"
Watching, waiting for the footsteps that will never come.
In "Southern prisons" pining, meager, tattered, pale
and gaunt,
Growing weaker, weaker daily from pinching cold
and want—
Are husbands, sons and brothers who hopeless
captives lie,
And ye who yet can save us—Will you leave us
here to die?

From out our prison gate there's a graveyard close
at hand,
Where lay fourteen thousand Union men beneath
a Southern sand,

And scores are laid beside them as day succeeds each day,
And thus it shall be until we all shall pass away;
And the last can say while dying with upturned glazing eye,
Both faith and love are dead at home and they've left us here to die.

---

18. At the end of each stanza, Comfort speaks to "ye who yet can save us." To whom is he probably speaking?
   F. Captain Henry Wirz
   G. Northern political leaders
   H. his fellow prisoners
   J. his prison guards

19. In line 2, the poet uses the phrase "broken ranks to fill." By this, he probably means that
   A. new soldiers must take the place of those who have died in the war
   B. Northern soldiers must repair worn-out military equipment
   C. many families have lost fathers and sons as a result of the war
   D. it seems the war will never end

20. Which expression uses figurative language to capture the effects of imprisonment?
   F. "Pinching cold and want"
   G. "A graveyard close at hand"
   H. "Our quiet happy home"
   J. "The scars upon our bodies"

21. Who would have been most likely to deny the factual accuracy of this poem?
   A. Comfort's family members
   B. Captain Henry Wirz
   C. The United States military court
   D. Soldiers imprisoned with William Comfort

22. According to the poem's second stanza, certain remarks made about the prisoners are untrue. Which statement would complete this chart?

True Remarks	False Remarks
We have tried to do our duty.	Our hearts are weak with fear.
_____?_____	We were captured from behind.

    F. We have been treated well by our captors.
    G. We have had regular contact with our families.
    H. Many among us have lost limbs during the war.
    J. We are confident that we will survive this imprisonment.

23. What was probably William Comfort's purpose in writing this poem?
    A. To help rally the other prisoners' spirits
    B. To appeal to Captain Wirz for relief from the horrible conditions at Andersonville
    C. To reveal the cruelty of the prison guards
    D. To encourage Northern officials to arrange their release

24. Which word best captures the mood of this poem?
    F. despair
    G. concern
    H. optimism
    J. amazement

25. Which of these best explains why each stanza ends with *nearly* the same line?
    A. The poet wants to emphasize his desperate plea for help.
    B. The poet wants to maintain the rhyme scheme.
    C. Most poems written during that era followed this form.
    D. The poem was written over years of imprisonment.

26. The tone of the poem's last stanza can best be described as:
- **F.** understated
- **G.** optimistic
- **H.** joyous
- **J.** cynical

Answers to Practice Reading Comprehension Section

1. C	7. D	12. H	17. B	22. H
2. F	8. H	13. A	18. G	23. D
3. C	9. B	14. G	19. A	24. F
4. F	10. F	15. D	20. F	25. A
5. D	11. C	16. J	21. B	26. J
6. G				

TIPS FOR TEACHERS

1. Do a reading comprehension multiple-choice Do Now.
2. Allow students to select their own reading passages from books, magazines, or online sources—whatever they happen to be reading. Then ask them to create their own multiple-choice questions. Analyze students' answers to these questions.
3. Make sure students are familiar with basic literary terms and devices—plot, conflict, setting, theme, foreshadowing, irony, symbolism, character, figurative language, rhyme, and so forth.
4. Introduce students to a variety of genres. Previous exams included nonfiction, fiction, poetry, memoir, and even an interview.
5. Different questions test different reading abilities—getting the main idea, understanding supporting details, determining cause and effect, making inferences and drawing conclusions, and understanding language from context clues and etymology. As you use this book and as students attempt similar reading activities, ask them to identify the skills required by each question.
6. Metacognition's the thing nowadays—and what a good thing it is! Have your students explain in writing why they have chosen a particular multiple-choice response and rejected the others.

7. Read aloud to your students, and have them read aloud to each other. Ask them to talk about the books they are reading. Middle school students care what their peers think. Seeing a merely popular book become an overnight sensation once word gets out is not unusual!

TIPS FOR PARENTS

1. "Do as I do." Studies have repeatedly demonstrated that readers beget readers. If your children have grown up in a home where their parents are avid readers, they are more likely to become readers themselves.

2. Be prepared to accept compromises. If your children enjoy reading the sports pages or teen magazines, do not waste too much energy insisting they read the classics. In the long run, you will not win that fight.

3. In a similar vein, some excellent young adult literature is being written these days—that may not have been the case when you were growing up. So do not be at all dismayed if your child is devouring the complete works of S. E. Hinton, Lois Duncan, or J. K. Rowling.

4. Your child's teachers should be requiring nightly reading assignments, either from a text the entire class is reading or from an outside reading text, usually chosen by the student. If this is not happening, you should find out why.

5. Recently, the New York State Department of Education recommended that all students read 25 books a year. Does your child's reading approach that figure? (By the way, reading is not the responsibility of the English teacher alone! All subject area teachers should be asking students to read and write.)

Chapter 2

Keys to Succeeding on the Listening-Writing Section

TWO ESSENTIAL SKILLS

Without a doubt, the Listening-Writing section of the New York State exam is the single component that will feel most alien to you. Yet, at the same time, it tests skills that are essential to succeeding not only in schools and colleges but also in the world beyond!

The following lists just a few of the kinds of listening activities and occasions you will surely encounter:

radio	television	films
tapes	songs	performances
meetings	lectures	presentations
discussions	orientations	sermons
directions	conversations	readings
guided tours	debates	political speeches
commercials	news reports	announcements

You listen selectively. You tend to listen most carefully when the subject matter is important to you. If you are a basketball fan, you will be listening very closely to the waning moments of a hotly contested game. As a teenager, you will probably want to listen very closely when your best friend phones or when you listen to news of current fashions or the hottest celebrities.

On the other hand, because you have heard it all before, you may respond indifferently to a parent's latest lecture on the relative merits of television watching and studying. Alternatively, when you fly in an airplane, you may tune out the pilot's directions for emergency procedures, because you are confident that your journey will not require them. (Let us hope you are right!)

Quite often, you will find yourself in situations that require you to listen closely, whether you are interested or not. As a college student, you may not be a lover of botany. However, because you will care a great deal about the grade you will receive in that course, you will decide to pay close attention during botany lectures. Later, as a member of the working world, you will understand the importance of listening carefully during meetings and presentations. You already know that families function better when members listen carefully.

Every now and then you hear about people with amazing memories, people who can recall with great accuracy every detail of a written work or spoken presentation. However, people with these photographic memories are few and far between. Most people need to write things down, which is why note taking is such an important skill.

THE TASK

The Grade 8 English Language Arts Exam will require you to listen to either one extended or two briefer passages. After you have listened and taken notes, you will have 45 minutes to answer three short-answer questions and one extended-response question. (The time you will need to listen and take notes is not included in the 45 minutes.) The short-answer questions have typically been of two types. You will probably need to complete one graphic organizer and answer two open-ended questions, each requiring a paragraph-length response. The extended-response question requires an essay-type answer.

The listening passage or passages will run about 4 or 5 minutes.

Included in the exam booklet is a page of directions, which the proctor will review with you. Some terms or vocabulary words you may not know will be explained to you on this page.

You will have two chances to listen to the listening passages. So do not feel as if absolutely no room exists for error.

The directions will tell you that, as you listen to the passages, you "may" take notes at any time.

First of all, forget about that "may." *You definitely need to take notes.* Students who take no or few notes do not do nearly as well as students who take excellent notes. That is a proven fact.

What is the best strategy? Should you try to record as much information as you can during the first reading and then use the second to fill in what you missed? Or should you listen only to the first reading and then take notes during the second?

Given the choice, students prefer—by an overwhelming margin—the first option. Most students prefer to listen closely to the first reading, take as many notes as possible, and then use the second reading to fill in whatever they may have missed.

If you have done a really good job during the first reading, you will discover that you have very little work to do during the second. And that's O.K. But make sure you use the second reading to answer a few basic "main idea" questions:

- What are these passages about?
- What is their purpose? For example, do they attempt to inform, entertain, or persuade?
- What is the main idea that these passages attempt to convey?
- If there are two passages, how are the passages related? Does the first introduce the second? Does one complement the other by providing detailed examples? Does the second passage serve as a contrast to the first?

When you have satisfactorily answered these general questions, you have more than just a basic understanding of the passages. You are also now able to determine which information you need to record in your notes.

LISTENING AND TAKING NOTES

If you go to a baseball game, you may decide to keep score, which is really nothing more than a highly specialized way of taking notes. Keeping score is very easy because you already know all the required symbols, and an outline (that is, a box score) has already been given to you.

Other situations offer similar note-taking aids. If you attend a well-prepared lecture, the lecturer has probably organized his or her material from an outline, and thus you will be able to discern the structure of the presentation. (Some lecturers distribute outlines—and notes—so all you need to do is fill in the gaps.) If you attend a meeting, you will be given an agenda, which lets you know which topics will be discussed.

The listening-writing section of the grade 8 exam is not so user-friendly. You will need to determine which information is important to record and how you wish to organize your notes. Here are a few helpful strategies to keep in mind:

- First of all, sit straight and tall; look directly at the reader.
- Stay focused during both readings. Do not think you can daydream through one reading and then catch it all during the second.
- The directions for the listening-writing section of the exam tell you that you "may" take notes. Do not be misled by this option. The booklet gives you at least a full page for notes; use this space.
- Decide ahead of time on your note-taking strategy. This text strongly suggests that you take notes during the first reading and fill in during the second. Make sure you understand the main idea and organization of each passage.
- Try to create some kind of graphic organizer in response to each passage's organization. For example, if you determine that the first passage is an introduction and the second a story, you might decide to create two columns. This way, your notes will line up side by side,

and you will be able to note similarities and differences between the two passages.

- Do not attempt to record information word for word. If you do, you will soon discover that, with every utterance, you are falling further and further behind.
- Write down what you feel to be an important point. Then, by using bullets or dashes, list details and examples under this main point.
- Pay attention to pauses, which may suggest that a new idea will follow.
- Listen for words that suggest importance: "cause," "result," and "reason" are just a few.
- Listen for words that suggest a series: "Twice before he had traveled to South America, once to Brazil and later to Colombia."
- Do not worry about words you do not know. Their meaning will probably become apparent as you understand the overall sense of the passages.
- When you take your notes, omit small words such as articles ("the," "a," and "an") and prepositions ("of," "to," and "from").
- Use symbols ($, &, #, ⇒) and abbreviations (e.g., etc., re) whenever possible.
- Develop your own shorthand. For example, use "NYC" for New York City or "Ody" for Odysseus.
- After you have finished listening to the second reading, check your notes to make sure you understand what you have recorded. Do this while the material is freshest in your mind. Make whatever corrections you deem necessary.
- As you review your notes, use asterisks (or underline) to denote important material.

These strategies are designed to help you record information quickly and thoroughly. Keep this simple principle in mind: The more notes you take, the easier it will be to perform well on this section of the test.

Apply these strategies to the following listening passages.

DIRECTIONS

In this part of the test, you will listen to two passages. The first is a speech given by Sojourner Truth. The second is an article about Betty Friedan. Then you will answer some questions to show how well you understood what was read.

You will listen to the speech and the article twice. As you listen carefully, you may take notes on both the introduction and the story anytime you wish during the readings. You may use these notes to answer the questions that follow. Use the space below and on page 63 for your notes.

Here are some words and definitions you may need to know as you listen:

- **out of kilter**   out of order
- **'twixt**   between
- **head**   beat
- **lash**   whip

(The listening selections can be found on pages 64–65.)

Notes

_____

_____

_____

_____

_____

_____

_____

_____

_____

_____

LISTENING SELECTION

Sojourner Truth was born into slavery in the state of New York in 1797. Thirty years later, when slavery was outlawed in New York, she began to travel around the country speaking about the rights of women and African-Americans. She delivered this speech in 1851 at a women's rights meeting in Akron, Ohio.

Well, children, where there is so much racket, there must be something out of kilter. I think that 'twixt the Negroes of the South and the women of the North, all talking about rights, the white men will be in a fix pretty soon. But what's all this here talking about?

That man over there says that women need to be helped into carriages, and lifted over ditches, and to have the best places everywhere. Nobody ever helps me into carriages, or over mud-puddles, or gives me any best place! And ain't I a woman? Look at me! Look at my arm. I have ploughed and planted and gathered into barns, and no man could head me! And ain't I a woman? I could work as much and eat as much as a man—when I could get it—bear the lash as well! And ain't I a woman? I have borne thirteen children, and have seen most all sold off to slavery, and when I cried out with my mother's grief, none but Jesus heard me! And ain't I a woman?

Then they talk about this thing in the head; what's this they call it? (Someone whispers, "Intellect.") That's it, honey. What's that got to do with women's rights or Negros' rights? If my cup won't hold but a pint, and yours holds a quart, wouldn't you be mean not to let me have my little half-measure full?

Then that little man in black there, he says women can't have as much rights as men, 'cause Christ wasn't a woman! Where did your Christ come from? From God and a woman! Man had nothing to do with Him.

If the first woman God ever made was strong enough to turn the world upside down all alone, these women together ought to be able to turn it back, and get it right side up again! And now they is asking to do it, the men better let them.

Obliged to you for hearing me, and now old Sojourner ain't got nothing more to say.

Journalist Betty Friedan's mother was herself a journalist who was forced to give up her career for marriage. When Betty was much younger, she turned down a college scholarship because her boyfriend believed it would end their relationship. Years later, Friedan became pregnant with her second child and was fired from her job as a reporter. These kinds of experiences were common among the women that Friedan spoke to. However, when she started to write articles about what women's lives were really like, she found that magazines would not publish these since advertisers liked the idea of happy, satisfied women buying their products.

In 1963, Betty Friedan published *The Feminine Mystique.* In this groundbreaking book, she exploded the myth that all women were happy homemakers. Instead, Friedan claimed, women were second-class citizens who had ignored their own emotional and intellectual needs in order to focus all their energies on caring for the needs of their husbands and children. And, she added, any woman who voiced her displeasure with this arrangement was said to be poorly adjusted, a "neurotic."

After the publication of her book, Friedan received thousands of letters from women, thanking her for putting into words what they had experienced for so long. Friedan began to travel and lecture. Everywhere she went, women spoke to her about injustices to women, and Friedan soon began to feel that talk was not enough.

In 1966, Friedan and a group of women and men founded the National Organization for Women, or NOW. NOW became a powerful organization in the battle for women's rights, tackling some very thorny issues. For example, because of pressure from NOW, the telephone company had to pay large sums of money to women to make up for years of paying higher wages to men for the same work. NOW argued for better child care facilities so that women could leave their homes and join the workplace. In 1971, before resigning as President of NOW, Friedan organized a Women's Strike for Equality. Fifty thousand women joined hands and marched down Fifth Avenue in New York City.

Compare your notes to these:

Sojourner Truth	Betty Friedan
Background • born slave NY, 1797 • 1827. Slav outlawed, speaks on women's, Afr-Am rights Man's pov: women helped into carriages, over ditches, best places everywhere But not for Soj! • Plowed, planted, gathered into barns • Work, eat like man • Bear the lash • Borne 13 ch, most sold to slavery, cried • Intellect: pint and quart • Christ not woman, but came from one • 1st woman (Eve) turned world upside down; then these can get it right again	Early exp • mother jrnl—give up career 4 marriage • B refused coll sch—boyfriend • B preg w/ 2nd ch—fired as reporter • These exp comon among women BF talked to 1963: _The Fem Mystique_ • Wom not happy homemakers • 2nd cl citizens ignore own needs 4 husb and ch • protesters "neurotic" • 1000s letters thank her NOW—powerful org 4 women's rights • phone co. pays $ 4 yrs of higher $ to men • better ch care facilities ⇒ women lv homes, work • Women's Strike for Equality, 5th Ave, NYC

For such an activity, so dependent upon individual judgments and shorthand codes, it would be highly unusual for two people to have identical notes. Your notes may differ from these and still be entirely adequate to your purposes. What is important for you to observe about this particular set of notes is its use of shorthand devices (abbreviations, symbols), its omission of small, unimportant words, and its tendency to clump information, almost as an outline does.

As you line up your two note pages, what similarities do you notice? Try to draw lines connecting related information. (For example, you should notice that both passages contain information about the backgrounds of Truth and Friedan.) Taking this extra step will help you prepare for the questions that follow.

SHORT-ANSWER QUESTIONS

The Listening-Writing section of the exam consists of three short-answer questions and one extended-response question. This section will generate two scores. The first, pertaining only to listening-writing skills, will be a holistic grade. That is, your answers to the four questions will not be graded individually; they will be read and evaluated as a whole. Your work on the extended-response question will also contribute to your overall writing conventions (that is, spelling, capitalization, grammar, and punctuation) score.

You will have 45 minutes to complete this section (in addition to the time needed to listen to the passages). For most students, that will be more than enough. Be sure, however, that you use your time wisely. Work carefully, and check your work when you have finished.

Before you answer some short-answer questions, keep in mind some helpful strategies:

- You should be familiar with graphic organizers because you will almost certainly see one on this section.
- Pay extremely close attention to directions. Be sure to distinguish between singular ("list an advantage") and plural ("in what ways") terms. Also, notice that some questions refer to one of the passages, while others require you to consider both.
- Undoubtedly, you have learned a great deal about writing good body paragraphs—about the importance of having a strong topic sentence followed by pertinent supporting sentences. On this section of the exam, some questions will require you to put this knowledge to use. Your response will be evaluated based on your understanding of the material. Therefore, you will need a topic sentence that goes beyond a mere repetition of the question. Write a topic sentence that shows you have been able to reach a conclusion about the passages you have heard. Follow this sentence with details and examples to illustrate your points.
- Do not be misled by the size of the space given to you to record your answers. Do not feel that you need to limit your answer to the five or six lines provided in the

exam booklet. By the same token, do not feel that you must write on every line or fill every box. Answer each question fully; elaborate as you see fit. If you need to use additional space, go right ahead.

■ Use your notes. It would be a pity, indeed, to have recorded important information in your notes only to omit these details from your answers.

Now, see how well you can apply these strategies to these short-answer questions.

1. Why does Sojourner Truth believe that she is the equal of most men? Use details from the passage to support your answer.

_____

_____

_____

_____

_____

2. Betty Friedan's personal experiences helped shape her position on the rights of women. Complete the chart below to show what Betty Friedan probably learned from one of these experiences.

An Early Experience	What Betty Learned

3. Betty Friedan's book *The Feminine Mystique* "exploded the myth that all women were happy home-makers." Yet she also came to understand that some people resisted this message: they did not wish to have this myth "exploded." In what ways is this resistance evident from the passage? Use details from the passage to support your answer.

_____

_____

_____

_____

_____

Now look at these model responses:

1. Why does Sojourner Truth believe that she is the equal of most men? Use details from the passage to support your answer.

Sojourner Truth believes she is the equal of most men because she has survived experiences that would test the character of just about any man. For example, in her speech she says that she has worked just as hard as any man, doing the plowing and planting on a farm. She also says that she has been forced to suffer as much as any man has. Two examples of this are being whipped as a slave and seeing her children sold off into slavery.

> *Commentary.* Notice that the response begins with a strong topic sentence, one that directly addresses the question and demonstrates insight into the material. Then, the writer cites two ways that Sojourner feels she is the equal of any man: she works as hard as a man, and she has suffered as much. However, the writer goes further than that, using specific references from the passage, supplying the kinds of details that "prove" one's points. Also, notice how all this material was taken directly from the notes.

2. Betty Friedan's personal experiences helped shape her position on the rights of women. Complete the chart below to show what Betty Friedan probably learned from one of these experiences.

An Early Experience	What Betty Learned
Betty did not accept a scholarship because her boyfriend said it would ruin their relationship.	Betty probably learned that women sometimes ignore their own needs because men want them to. She probably learned that this is a bad idea.

> *Commentary.* First of all, the question calls for one personal experience. This writer selected one pertaining to Betty's education; you could have chosen others. The question requires you to think critically about how this experience might have shaped her attitudes and beliefs about the women's rights issue. This response concludes that Betty, after having sacrificed an educational opportunity in order to satisfy her boyfriend's wishes, probably realized that women often make these kinds of sacrifices—to their own detriment. This is a sensible conclusion to draw.

3. Betty Friedan's book *The Feminine Mystique* "exploded the myth that all women were happy home-makers." Yet she also came to understand that some people resisted this message: they did not wish to have this myth "exploded." In what ways is this resistance evident from the passage? Use details from the passage to support your answer.

Betty Friedan wanted to "explode" the myth that women are all happy homemakers, but she soon learned that men did not want to have this myth proven false. Early in her career as a journalist, she began to write stories about women's real lives. However, she soon discovered that magazines would not print these since the advertisers wanted happy women buyers for their products. Later, in her book The Feminine Mystique, Friedan talked about the way men reacted to women who complained about their condition. They said these women were poorly adjusted neurotics, which sort of placed the blame onto the women for complaining.

Commentary. You will notice that this full, complete answer probably could not be squeezed into the six lines that the booklet provides, so do not worry about that! The response begins with a good topic sentence. More important in this case, it offers an insightful discussion of two ways that men were eager to maintain the "happy homemaker" myth. Once again, all this material was taken directly from the notes.

THE EXTENDED-RESPONSE QUESTION

"Extended response" is the latest term for essay, which you have been writing throughout your middle school career. So by now, you know that the key to good essay writing is organization, taking time to decide how you will present the material you know.

Before we take a look at the actual extended-response question, review some useful strategies:

- The exam gives you a page for planning. Use it—at the very least to outline your body paragraphs.
- Use your notes in the planning process.
- You may use material from the short-answer section to write your extended response. Sometimes the short-answer section will include a question that helps you build your extended response. Don't feel like you're copying if you have to use the same ideas twice.
- Provide an introduction that states the essay's main idea and suggests its organization. Allow the question to dictate the essay's structure. Do not automatically "plug in" to a comfortable structure; instead, think about how you should organize your answer.
- Provide a conclusion that summarizes or highlights the essay's main points.
- Once again, writing good body paragraphs is paramount. Use comprehensive topic sentences and apt examples to prove your points.
- Make sure you have addressed all of the bulleted items in the question. Failing to do this will certainly result in your receiving a lower grade.
- This section of the test *usually* does not seek information about your personal opinions or experiences. But "usually" is not the same as "always" or "never," so be alert to that possibility. Read the question carefully to determine precisely what is asked of you.
- Once again, do not feel limited by the space assigned. If you wish to write more, just make sure you have marked all sections carefully.
- Recognize the "conventions" icon when you see it. Be sure to check your grammar, spelling, punctuation, and paragraphs.

Now, examine the extended-response question:

4. Both Sojourner Truth and Betty Friedan "talk the talk" and "walk the walk." In other words, they demonstrate their beliefs about women's rights not only through what they say but also through their experiences and actions.

Discuss how Sojourner Truth and Betty Friedan have demonstrated their beliefs about women's rights through words and actions. Use information from both passages to support your response.

In your answer, be sure to include

■ how Betty Friedan and Sojourner Truth have demonstrated their beliefs about women's rights through words
■ how Betty Friedan and Sojourner Truth have demonstrated their beliefs about women's rights through experiences and actions
■ details from BOTH listening passages

 Check your writing for correct spelling, grammar, and punctuation.

Before you tackle this question, think about how you will organize your outline and your answer. You will probably conclude that this question requires a four-paragraph response, which might look like this:

1. introduction
2. body paragraph 1 (Sojourner Truth)
3. body paragraph 2 (Betty Friedan)
4. conclusion

This is the most obvious way—and perhaps the easiest way, as well—to structure your essay. You simply allocate one body paragraph to the Sojourner Truth section of the listening passage and another to Betty Friedan. This is an entirely acceptable strategy. Should you use it, you could write an exemplary essay.

Another, equally acceptable strategy would be as follows:

1. introduction
2. body paragraph 1 (words: "talks the talk")
3. body paragraph 2 (experiences, actions: "walks the walk")
4. conclusion

In this case, you would be following the structure offered by the question. Either organization is perfectly acceptable. The true quality of your response will lie in your ability to develop your essay with suitable details.

 Note: Make sure you check out Chapter 4. It provides additional tips on composition writing, language use, and conventions.

Now, by using one of these strategies, answer the extended-response question.

PLANNING PAGE

You may PLAN your writing for question 4 here if you wish, but do NOT write your final answer on this page. Your writing on this Planning Page will NOT count toward your final score. Write your final answer beginning on the next page.

4. Both Sojourner Truth and Betty Friedan "talk the talk" and "walk the walk." In other words, they demonstrate their beliefs about women's rights not only through what they say but also through their experiences and actions.

Discuss how Sojourner Truth and Betty Friedan have demonstrated their beliefs about women's rights through words and actions. Use information from both passages to support your response.

In your answer, be sure to include

■ how Betty Friedan and Sojourner Truth have demonstrated their beliefs about women's rights through words

■ how Betty Friedan and Sojourner Truth have demonstrated their beliefs about women's rights through experiences and actions

■ details from BOTH listening passages

Check your writing for correct spelling, grammar, and punctuation.

_____

_____

_____

_____

_____

_____

_____

_____

_____

_____

_____

MODEL EXTENDED RESPONSE

This model extended response uses the first strategy discussed earlier (a paragraph about Truth, another about Friedan). The writer, noticing that his or her notes contained more information about experiences and actions, decided to write two body paragraphs of equal length rather than one brief paragraph about words and one longer one about actions and experiences.

The writer then created an outline that looks like this:

Truth's earlier experiences convinced her to speak about women's rights
- earlier experiences as slave (lash, mother w/ kids sold into slavery)
- earlier experiences as laborer on farm
- travels country speaking about women's rights
- first woman (Eve) turned world upside down; now women can fix it!

Friedan learns that words not enough; must act
- writer on women's rights (earlier for magazines, then Fem Myst)
- NOW: phone company/wages to women
- NOW: better child care facilities/women work
- Women's Strike for Equality

Notice that this outline of the essay's body section contains headings followed by a series of examples. Each heading suggests a topic sentence, one that will be well supported by the examples that follow.

Here is the essay itself:

Sojourner Truth and Betty Friedan are two women who "talk the talk" and "walk the walk." These two outspoken women combine words with actions in their approaches to dealing with women's rights issues.

Sojourner Truth's harsh experiences earlier in her life convinced her that women were equal to men. Sojourner Truth suffered a great deal as a slave, having to bear the whip and, even worse, seeing many of her 13 children taken from her and sold into slavery. As a woman working on a farm, she discovered that, when it came to the chores of the farm, like plowing and planting, she could work as hard as any man. She felt that women became stronger through their suffering. Later in her life, when she crossed the country speaking about the rights of women, she communicated these ideas. She spoke confidently of women's abilities, saying that since a woman like Eve was strong enough to mess up everything in the first place, women were also certainly strong enough to set it all right.

As a writer, Betty Friedan wrote articles and a book (The Feminine Mystique) about how women were not happy homemakers but actually second-class citizens who often sacrificed their own happiness for the happiness of their husbands and children. Even though many women admired her written work, Friedan discovered that words were not enough. She became one of the founders of the National Organization for Women. NOW fought for women's rights, forcing the telephone company to pay large sums of money to women to make up for years of having paid larger salaries to men. Friedan and NOW also fought for better child care facilities so that women could return to the world of work. Before she retired as NOW's president, she led a huge Women's Strike for Equality; more than 50,000 women marched down Fifth Avenue in New York City.

Because they were able to "talk the talk" and "walk the walk," Betty Friedan and Sojourner Truth became important figures in the women's rights movement. Truth knew that her experiences qualified her to talk about women's rights. Friedan also realized that while words could be powerful, they sometimes were not enough.

Commentary. This essay succeeds because it answers the question directly and convincingly, using many details from both the passages to prove its points. It addresses all the question's requirements. Notice also how closely the response follows the outline. However, it does not follow the outline exactly—nor should it, as an outline is merely a plan. Can you see where the essay differs from the outline?

TIPS FOR PARENTS

Yes, parents, you can help your child succeed on the Listening-Writing section! Here are a few examples of activities you can do together:

1. Read aloud to each other. If, for example, you come across something interesting in the newspaper, say, "Listen to this," and read a portion to your child. Have your child do the same for you. Then discuss what you have read/heard.
2. Ask your child about the lyrics of a song he or she is listening to. (Given today's lyrics, you may need to exercise some care with this one!)
3. Watch TV together. A sound activity for other reasons, this also furnishes an excellent listening opportunity. Once again, discuss what you have heard and seen.
4. Books on cassette are an excellent way to pass time on a long car trip. (Of course, choosing a work of mutual interest may not be easy.) Discuss!
5. Cultural activities offer a myriad of listening opportunities—guided tours, audio tours, lectures. Avail yourself of these.

Above all, listen to your child; in so doing, you will foster an environment conducive to listening. We all know that teenagers expect us to listen when they have something to say. Though their timing is sometimes less than ideal, it is imperative that we listen right then and there. When children know we care enough to drop what we are doing to hear their concerns, they will be more likely to listen to ours.

TIPS FOR TEACHERS

Listening-writing opportunities abound and can easily be incorporated into your existing class structure. You know that a good teacher varies lesson formats; include a variety of listening activities in your lessons. A few suggestions and guidelines to keep in mind:

1. Teach note taking from oral sources. Make sure your listening activities have a note-taking component.
2. Read aloud to your students; have your students read aloud to each other.
3. Lecture. This ultratraditional activity still has its place in the classroom. Besides, if students are asked to take notes, it is highly student centered.
4. Oral presentations (as well as video ones) are especially effective when students are held accountable for what they have heard.
5. Teach outlining. This essential critical thinking skill requires students to classify facts and concepts.
6. Turn your Do Now into a listening activity.
7. Dictation. This activity, as old as the hills, is useful in small doses. Why not dictate the homework assignment once in a while instead of writing it onto the board?
8. You cannot overestimate the importance of a good reader. Give yourself practice reading aloud. Familiarize yourself, as well as other readers, with the passage. Read at a reasonable pace and with appropriate expression.

Above all, listening-writing is not the responsibility of the English Language Arts teacher alone! Familiarize your colleagues in other departments (school administrators, too!) with this section of the exam. Help them to see how these skills are essential to their subjects, too. Help them to develop appropriate activities.

ANOTHER SAMPLE LISTENING ACTIVITY

DIRECTIONS

You will listen to two passages. The first is an introduction. It will tell you about an author and will give you some background information about a piece he wrote. The second passage will be the piece itself. You will answer some questions to show how well you understood what was read.

You will listen to the selection twice. As you listen carefully, you may take notes anytime you wish. You may use these notes to answer the questions that follow.

Here are some terms and definitions you may need to know as you listen:

- **swindled**   cheated
- **a heap**   by far
- **blackguarding** insulting
- **aholt of**   holding onto

Notes

_____

_____

_____

_____

_____

_____

_____

_____

_____

_____

INTRODUCTION

Samuel Clemens, better known as Mark Twain, is one of the nation's best-loved and most widely read authors. In what is perhaps his most famous novel, The Adventures of Huckleberry Finn, *Twain created a character whose fictional experiences enabled the author to comment on his observations of the Americans he came to know.*

Though Twain may be associated almost automatically with the wholesome humor of Tom Sawyer's practical jokes, many critics believe that his best works are those in which he satirizes—or criticizes, even ridicules—the behavior of his fellow Americans. His satire could be directed in two different directions. Sometimes, Twain would criticize the behavior of individuals, believing they could be unfeeling and cruel. At other times, he satirized the behavior of the mob, suggesting that, even if individuals were themselves good hearted and caring, their worst instincts usually prevailed when they gathered in groups.

SELECTION

In this passage from *The Adventures of Huckleberry Finn,* Huck has arrived in a small town and now observes an incident involving two men, Boggs, the loud-mouthed but harmless town drunk, and Colonel Sherburne, a man Boggs has accused of cheating him. Equally important, however, is the reaction of the townspeople to this incident.

Boggs rode up before the biggest store in town and bent his head down so he could see under the curtain of the awning, and yells—

"Come out here, Sherburn! Come out and meet the man you've swindled. You're the houn[d] I'm after, and I'm gwyne to have you, too!"

And so he went on, calling Sherburn everything he could lay his tongue to, and the whole street packed with people listening and laughing and going on. By-and-by a proud-looking man about fifty-five—and he a heap the best dressed man in that town, too—steps out of the store, and the crowd drops back on each side to let him come. He says to Boggs, mighty ca'm and slow—he says:

"I'm tired of this; but I'll endure it till one o'clock. Till one o'clock, mind—no longer. If you open your mouth against me only once, after that time, you can't travel so far but I will find you."

Then he turns and goes in. The crowd looked mighty sober; nobody stirred, and there warn't no more laughing. Boggs rode off blackguarding Sherburn as loud as he could yell, all down the street; and pretty soon back he come and stops before the store, still keeping it up. Some men crowded around him and tried to get him to shut up, but he wouldn't; they told him it would be one o'clock in about fifteen minutes, and so he must go home—he must go right away. But it didn't do no good. He cussed away, with all his might, and throwed his hat down in the mud and rode over it, and pretty soon away he went a-raging down the street again, with his gray hair a-flying. Everybody that could get a chance at him tried their best to coax him off of his horse so they could lock him up and get him sober; but it warn't no use—up the street he would tear again, and give Sherburn another cussing. By-and-by somebody says—

"Go for his daughter!—quick, go for his daughter; sometimes he'll listen to her. If anybody can persuade him, she can."

So somebody started on a run. . . . In about five or ten minutes, here comes Boggs again—but not on his horse. He was a-reeling across the street . . . with a friend on both sides of him aholt of his arms and hurrying him along. He was quiet, and looked uneasy; and he . . . was doing some of the hurrying himself. Somebody sings out—

"Boggs!"

I looked over to see who said it, and it was that Colonel Sherburn. He was standing perfectly still, in the street, and had a pistol raised in his right hand—not aiming it, but holding it out with a barrel tilted up towards the sky. The same second I see a young girl coming on the run, and two men with her. Boggs and the men turn around, to see who called him, and when they see the pistol the men jumped to one side, and the pistol barrel came down slow and steady to a level—both barrels cocked. Boggs throws up both of his hands, and says, "O Lord, don't shoot!" Bang! goes the first shot, and he staggers back clawing at the air—bang! goes the second one, and he tumbles backwards onto the ground heavy and solid, with his arms spread out. That young girl screamed out, and comes rushing, and down she throws herself on her father, crying, and saying, "Oh, he's killed him, he's killed him!" The crowd closed up around them, and shouldered and jammed one another, with their necks stretched, trying to see, and people on the inside trying to shove them back, and shouting, "Back back! Give him air, give him air!"

Colonel Sherburn he tossed his pistol onto the ground, and turned around on his heels and walked off.

They took Boggs to a little drug store, the crowd pressing around, just the same, and the whole town following, and I rushed and got a good place at the window, where I was close to him and could see in. They laid him on the floor. . . . He made about a dozen long gasps . . . and after that he laid still; he was dead. Then they pulled his daughter away from him, screaming and crying, and took her off. She was about sixteen, and very sweet and gentle-looking, but awful pale and scared.

Well, pretty soon the whole town was there, squirming and . . . pushing and shoving to get at the window and have a look, but people that had the places wouldn't give them up, and folks behind them was saying all the time, "Say, now, you've looked enough, you fellows; 'taint right and 'taint fair, for you to stay thar all the time, and never give nobody a chance; other folks has their rights as well as you."

---

1. From this passage emerges a brief portrait of Boggs. Complete the chart on page 88, indicating both a character trait and details from the passage that support that character trait.

Boggs' Character Trait	Details from the Passage

2. The first thing that Huck notices about Sherburne is that he's a "proud-looking man." Is Huck's first impression correct? Use details from the passage to support your opinion.

_____

_____

_____

_____

_____

3. How does the behavior of the townspeople change once they realize that Boggs is in genuine danger? Use details from the passage to support your answer.

_____

_____

_____

_____

_____

PLANNING PAGE

You may PLAN your writing for question 4 here if you wish, but do NOT write your final answer on this page. Your writing on this Planning Page will NOT count toward your final score. Write your final answer beginning on the next page.

4. Satire can be defined as a literary work that holds up human faults to ridicule or scorn. How does Mark Twain expose the faults of individuals and groups in this passage from *Huckleberry Finn*? Use information from the introduction and passage in your answer.

   In your answer, be sure to include

   ■ examples of individuals' faults that Twain ridicules
   ■ examples of group behavior that Twain ridicules
   ■ information from the introduction and the listening passage

Check your writing for correct spelling, grammar, and punctuation.

_____

_____

_____

_____

_____

_____

_____

_____

_____

_____

_____

_____

_____

_____

_____

Chapter 3

Keys to Succeeding on the Reading-Writing Section

THE TASK

The Reading-Writing section of the exam is the third and final section. It is administered on the second day of testing. You will have a full 60 minutes to complete the Reading-Writing section.

The Reading-Writing section very closely resembles the Listening-Writing section. First, both usually offer two linked passages. Second, you will be asked to complete three short-answer questions and one extended-answer (essay) question.

Here are some general strategies that will help you perform well on this section of the exam:

- Read actively. This simply means that you need to interact with the text. As you are reading, ask yourself the usual questions. What is the author trying to say? What is the author's purpose in writing this passage? How does the author use details to get across the main idea? By all means, feel free to write in your booklet. Underline important passages or words; write in the margins.
- Look carefully at the title and accompanying graphics—photos and captions, for example—because these may contain information that you can use in your answers.
- Just as you did for the previous sections, pay close attention to the directions. If you are asked to "identify

information from the story," then one piece of information will do. However, if you are asked to "use details from the story," then you will need to supply more than one supporting detail. Also, notice that some questions refer to one of the passages, while others require you to consider both.

▪ Once again, remember to use what you have learned about writing good body paragraphs—about the importance of having a strong topic sentence followed by pertinent supporting sentences. On this section of the exam, some questions will require you to put this knowledge to use. Your response will be evaluated based on your understanding of the material and your ability to use details and examples to illustrate your points.

▪ Again, do not be misled by the size of the space given to you to record your answers. Do not feel that you need to limit your answer to the five or six lines provided in the exam booklet. By the same token, do not feel that you must write on every line or fill every box. Answer each question fully; elaborate as you see fit. If you need to use additional space, go right ahead.

Apply these strategies to the first passage.

DIRECTIONS

In this part of the test, you are going to read an excerpt from Stephen Crane's novel *The Red Badge of Courage*. Then you will answer questions about the piece. You may look back at the piece as often as you like.

This excerpt has been taken from an early chapter of Stephen Crane's novel of the Civil War, *The Red Badge of Courage*. Henry Fielding, the novel's main character, has just enlisted in the Army of the North, and he is about to go off to war.

One night, as he lay in bed, the winds had carried to him the clang-oring of the church bell as some enthusiast jerked the rope franti-cally to tell the twisted news of a great battle. This voice of the people rejoicing in the night had made him shiver in a prolonged ecstasy of excitement. Later, he had gone down to his mother's room and had spoken thus: "Ma, I'm going to enlist."

"Henry, don't you be a fool," his mother had replied. She had then covered her face with the quilt. There was an end to the matter for that night.

Nevertheless, the next morning he had gone to a town that was near his mother's farm and had enlisted in a company that was forming there. When he had returned home his mother was milking the brindle cow. Four others stood waiting. "Ma, I've enlisted," he had said to her diffidently.[1] There was a short silence. "The Lord's will be done, Henry," she had finally replied, and had then con-tinued to milk the brindle cow.

When he had stood in the doorway with his soldier's clothes on his back, and with the light of excitement and expectancy in his eyes almost defeating the glow of regret for the home bonds, he had seen two tears leaving their trails on his mother's scarred cheeks.

Still, she had disappointed him by saying nothing whatever about returning with his shield or on it. He had privately primed[2] himself for a beautiful scene. He had prepared certain sentences which he thought could be used with touching effect. But her words destroyed his plans. She had doggedly peeled potatoes and addressed him as follows: "You watch out, Henry, an' take good care of yerself in this here fighting business—you watch out, an' take good care of yerself. Don't go a-thinkin' you can lick the hull[3] rebel army at the start, because yeh can't. Yer just one little feller amongst a hull lot of others, and yeh've got to keep quiet an' do what they tell yeh. I know how you are, Henry.

"I've knet yeh eight pairs of socks, Henry, and I've put in all yer best shirts, because I want my boy to be jest as warm and com'able

[1]**diffidently:** shyly
[2]**primed:** readied
[3]**hull:** whole

as anybody in the army. Whenever they get holes in 'em, I want yeh to send 'em right-away back to me, so's I kin dern[4] 'em.

"An' allus[5] be careful an' choose yer comp'ny. There's lots of bad men in the army, Henry. The army makes 'em wild, and they like nothing better than the job of leading off a young feller like you, as ain't never been away from home much and has allus had a mother, an' a-learning 'em to drink and swear. Keep clear of them folks, Henry. I don't want yeh to ever do anything, Henry, that yeh would be 'shamed to let me know about. Jest think as if I was a 'watch' yeh. If yeh keep that in yer mind allus, I guess yeh'll come out about right. . . ."

He had, of course, been impatient under the ordeal of this speech. It had not been quite what he expected, and he had borne it with an air of irritation. He departed feeling vague relief.

Still, when he had looked back from the gate, he had seen his mother kneeling among the potato parings. Her brown face, upraised, was stained with tears, and her spare form was quivering. He bowed his head and went on, feeling suddenly ashamed of his purposes.

Now answer these two short-answer questions:

1. Henry's mother says to him, "I know how you are, Henry." What character traits is she referring to? Complete the chart by listing the character trait and supporting details found in the passage.

Henry's Character Traits	Supporting Information

[4]**dern:** darn (repair)
[5]**allus:** always

2. Henry is disappointed that his farewell conversation with his mother did not go as he had hoped. Why did Henry find her words irritating? Use details from the passage to support your answer.

_____

_____

_____

_____

_____

Compare your answers to these model responses.

1. Henry's mother says to him, "I know how you are, Henry." What character traits is she referring to? Complete the chart by listing the character trait and supporting details found in the passage.

Henry's Character Traits	Supporting Information
Henry is naive.	He thinks war is exciting. He is not as aware of the dangers as he should be.
Henry is impressionable.	His mother has to warn him to stay away from the wrong types of men in the army.

Commentary. "Naive" and "impressionable" are two acceptable answers. You might also say that he is disobedient because he does not heed his mother's request that he not enlist. In fact, you could come up with a lot of different character traits. The point is that you also need to produce evidence from the passage that supports those character traits. The answers given above do just that.

2. Henry is disappointed that his farewell conversation with his mother did not go as he had hoped. Why did Henry find her words irritating? Use details from the passage to support your answer.

Henry had hoped that his farewell conversation with his mother would go a certain way, and then he was disappointed when it did not turn out that way at all. He was hoping that his mother would say something about his "returning with his shield or on it," meaning that either he would return a hero or die a hero. Instead, his mother warned him not to try to do too much at once, not to try too hard to act heroically. She reminded him of the need to act carefully. In a way, her words suggested to Henry that warm and comfortable clothes were more important than were any of his ideas about heroism, and he really did not want to hear that.

Commentary. This well-written paragraph answers the question directly and convincingly. Notice that it begins with two sentences that serve to express its main idea: Henry is concerned with heroism and drama, while his mother is concerned primarily with safety and caution. The paragraph develops that idea further by using—and explaining—a quote that sums up Henry's romantic notions. Then the paragraph goes on to give several examples of the mother's cautionary advice.

Try another prose passage.

Staying Home

My brother's friend Marty had been home from Vietnam for three weeks, but I hadn't seen him yet. He wasn't feeling well, my brother said; he wasn't feeling well enough to come out.

But one spring afternoon, I came home from high school and found Marty and my brother sitting on the couch in the living room. Marty looked the same, except his blond hair was cut short, army style.

I wasn't sure why Marty had enlisted since hardly anyone I knew was in any kind of hurry to go fight in Vietnam. Most people I knew objected to the war for one reason or another. One thing was for sure, though: every night televised images of boys dying in the jungle came into our living rooms, and Vietnam seemed just too scary a thing to seek on one's own.

Marty had just graduated from high school. Most guys in that situation simply went on to college, because college guaranteed a deferment. That seemed good enough since who knew what would happen four years from now? Maybe that crazy war would be over. But Marty didn't feel that way. In high school he had been an indifferent student, good in some subjects, but unwilling to apply himself fully. He was in no particular hurry to embrace another four years of classes, especially since he didn't know what he'd care to study or what he planned to do afterward. Besides, Marty had always been a little different. He didn't have very many friends. He was shy and awkward around people he didn't know. When he got excited about an idea or a book he had read, he stuttered and needed to catch his breath. My brother had said that Marty needed to find himself and maybe that would happen in the army, in Vietnam.

Now Marty sat on the couch and spoke about the heat and the insects of the jungle. He spoke about a night so black that we New York City folks couldn't even begin to imagine its absolute darkness. He spoke about young men dying, friends he had just made. Sometimes they died quickly, immediately, sometimes not. Sometimes they were ready to die. Usually, though, death just took them unprepared. Marty spoke about being so afraid that he couldn't speak, he couldn't make sense to anyone, so the army had no choice but to discharge him and send him home.

As he spoke, I listened closely. After a while it occurred to me that throughout his monologue I had heard something else, a noise—a slight knocking—in the background, and then I realized what it was. It was the ice cubes in his glass of soda, crashing against the side of the glass, as his hand shook uncontrollably.

Now answer the following question:

3. "My brother had said that Marty needed to find himself." Discuss the meaning of this expression. Do you think Marty was successful in this goal? Use details from the passage to support your answer.

_____

_____

_____

_____

_____

Compare your short-answer response to this model:

Marty needed to find himself because he was not too sure of who he was. In high school he had been a so-so student, and he was not very sure about his academic or career goals. Socially, he did not have too many friends, maybe because he was a little different from most people, uncertain of himself, shy, and awkward. He hoped he could find himself in Vietnam, but it does not sound as if that happened. Instead, he found a horrifying experience in Vietnam, one he could not deal with at all, so the army sent him home.

> *Commentary. This short answer clearly and directly addresses the question, first by stating what the expression means ("he wasn't too sure of who he was") and then citing details from the passage to provide further explanation. The response indicates that Marty had not found himself in Vietnam but had instead been overwhelmed by the difficulties he had encountered there.*

A SPECIAL CASE: POETRY

Of the two reading selections in this section, you can be certain that at least one will be prose. The second may also be prose, but it could be poetry, too. So you need to be prepared for that possibility.

When you looked closely at the reading comprehension chapter, you reviewed some poetic terms and devices, such as "rhyme," "personification," "simile," and "metaphor." Certainly, the ability to use appropriate terminology when discussing poetry could come in handy in the Reading-Writing section, too. However, this section of the exam is concerned primarily with meaning—with your ability to understand the poetry you read, to express these ideas in writing, and, ultimately, to relate these ideas to those expressed in the other work.

Accordingly, keep these principles in mind when you read poetry:

- Always pay attention to the introductory material, which often provides useful information.
- Difficult vocabulary will be defined for you. Look for these definitions.
- Read poetry from punctuation mark to punctuation mark—not from the beginning of the line to the end.

Notice these lines from Shakespeare's *Macbeth*:

> And all our yesterdays have lighted fools
> The way to dusty death.

These two lines together express a complete thought. Granted, it is a complex thought. However, you would be making a mistake to think that you should pause after "fools" since the idea (in this case, a sentence) continues on the next line.

- Read the poem slowly, focusing in your first reading on getting the main idea. Then, go back and read the poem a second time. As you do so, think about how all the pieces work toward expressing that main idea. What do we mean by pieces? They are lines and stanzas, for one thing, but also the poet's use of figurative language, rhyme, and so forth.
- Be aware of the difference between the narrator and the poet. The narrator is the character who is telling the story in a particular poem; the poet is the writer, the person who created the narrator.
- When you write about the poem, always use details from it to support your answer.

Now take a close look at Thomas Hardy's poem "The Man He Killed."

Had he and I but met
By some old ancient inn,
We should have sat us down to wet
Right many a nipperkin![1]

But ranged as infantry,[2]
And staring face to face,
I shot at him as he at me,
And killed him in his place.

I shot him dead because—
Because he was my foe,
Just so: my foe of course he was;
That's clear enough; although

He thought he'd 'list,[3] perhaps,
Off-hand-like[4]—just as I—
Was out of work—had sold his traps[5]—
No other reason why.

Yes; quaint and curious war is!
You shoot a fellow down
You'd treat, if met where any bar is,
Or help to half-a-crown.[6]

Now answer question 4.

[1]**nipperkin:** a half-pint cup (of beer)
[2]**infantry:** foot soldiers
[3]**'list:** enlist
[4]**off-hand-like:** without much thought
[5]**traps:** belongings
[6]**help to half-a-crown:** lend money to

4. What do you think is the poet's purpose in writing the poem? Use details from the poem to support your answer.

_____

_____

_____

_____

_____

_____

Examine this model answer.

In "The Man He Killed," Thomas Hardy is trying to show that war can be very troubling because a soldier must kill men he would probably be friends with during peacetime. That is just what happens in this poem. The narrator, an infantryman, meets a man in combat and, only because they are foes, he is forced to shoot at and kill him. The narrator realizes that that is the only reason for killing. On the other hand, he also realizes that the two men are probably similar, having enlisted for just about the same reason, and, had they met in peacetime, they would probably have shared a few drinks or even lent each other money.

> _Commentary. The response begins with a topic sentence in which the writer notes the antiwar theme of the poem. The rest of the response offers a clear explanation of the writer's purpose and includes lots of pertinent details—the similarities between the men, the drinks they might have had—that support the theme. A response of this length could not fit into the allotted space!_

THE EXTENDED-RESPONSE QUESTION

The extended-response (essay) question on the Listening-Writing section requires you to write about both passages (or the introduction and the main passage). This extended response will do the same in the Reading-Writing section.

The strategies you reviewed for the Listening-Writing extended response will serve you well here:

- The exam gives you a page for planning. Use it—at the very least to outline your body paragraphs.
- Use your notes in the planning process.
- Use material from the short-answer section. On this exam, the short-answer section helps you construct your extended response. Use hints from the questions and your answers. In fact, do not be reluctant to use large parts of your short answers in the extended response.
- Provide an introduction that states the essay's main idea and suggests its organization. Allow the question to dictate the essay's structure. Do not automatically plug in to a comfortable structure; instead, think about how you should organize your answer.
- Provide a conclusion that summarizes or highlights the essay's main points.
- Once again, writing good body paragraphs is paramount. Use comprehensive topic sentences and apt examples to prove your points.
- Bear in mind that this is *not* a personal-opinion question. You are expected to base your response entirely on the material from the reading passages. Do not include personal experiences or opinions in your response.
- Once again, do not feel limited by the space assigned. If you wish to write more, just make sure you have marked all sections carefully.
- Recognize the conventions icon when you see it. Be sure to check your grammar, spelling, punctuation, and paragraphs.

One more thing—and it is a very important thing—if one of the passages is a poem, you may be asked to choose a line or lines from the poem and to discuss the meaning of those lines. You may be asked, as well, to discuss how they apply to the other work. Be warned: this is a tricky task, and you need to give a great deal of thought to the lines you choose. So keep in mind these few basic, guiding principles:

- Choose lines that demonstrate the poem's main idea. (Do not choose lines that contain relatively minor details!) Not all poems state the main idea in so many words, so you will need to choose a section of the poem that you feel demonstrates the main idea.
- Choose lines that express a complete thought. Think in terms of complete sentences or, at least, an image or idea that can stand on its own.
- Familiarize yourself with the use of the ellipsis (. . .) as a device that will enable you to quote directly but, at the same time, to omit unneeded words or lines.
- In organizing your extended response, discuss the lines of poetry first; then show how they apply to the prose work. This will make for a clearer discussion.

With this in mind, take a crack at this question.

 Note: This extended-response question requires you to write about two of the reading passages in this chapter: the excerpt from Stephen Crane's *The Red Badge of Courage* and "The Man He Killed," Thomas Hardy's poem.

PLANNING PAGE

You may PLAN your writing for question 5 here if you wish, but do NOT write your final answer on this page. Your writing on this Planning Page will NOT count toward your final score. Write your final answer beginning on the next page.

5. Choose a line or lines from Thomas Hardy's poem "The Man He Killed." Discuss the meaning of these lines, and explain how they apply to the scene involving Henry Fielding and his mother. Use ideas from both the poem and *The Red Badge of Courage* in your answer.

In your answer, be sure to include

- the line or lines you have selected from the poem
- an explanation of how this selection applies to Henry Fielding and his mother

Check your writing for correct spelling, grammar, and punctuation.

_____

_____

_____

_____

_____

_____

_____

_____

_____

_____

_____

_____

_____

_____

_____

See how this model extended response compares with yours.

PLANNING PAGE

You may PLAN your writing for question 5 here if you wish, but do NOT write your final answer on this page. Your writing on this Planning Page will NOT count toward your final score. Write your final answer beginning on the next page.

> Yes; quaint and curious war is!
> You shoot a fellow down
> You'd treat, if met where any bar is,
> Or help to half-a-crown.

- narrator understands in mature way the nature of war
- unfortunately, kill or be killed, but otherwise nothing personal against foe
- in fact, would probably be friends

The Red Badge of Courage

- Mother comes closer to understanding than Hardy's narrator has reached
- sees enlisting as "fool" thing to do
- more concerned with Henry's not doing something foolishly brave, but risky
- more concerned with simple things like keeping warm

- Henry has romantic attitude toward war
- Church bell = excitement of war
- imagines dramatic farewell speech to mom
- eventually realizes how his enlisting causing mom to suffer

5. Choose a line or lines from Thomas Hardy's poem "The Man He Killed." Discuss the meaning of these lines, and explain how they apply to the scene involving Henry Fielding and his mother. Use ideas from both the poem and *The Red Badge of Courage* in your answer.

In your answer, be sure to include

■ the line or lines you have selected from the poem
■ an explanation of how this selection applies to Henry Fielding and his mother

 Check your writing for correct spelling, grammar, and punctuation.

War is the subject of much of literature. In Thomas Hardy's poem "The Man He Killed" and an excerpt from Stephen Crane's novel <u>The Red Badge of Courage</u>, different characters feel very differently about the subject of war.

Hardy's poem includes these lines:

> Yes; quaint and curious war is!
> You shoot a fellow down
> You'd treat, if met where any bar is,
> Or help to half-a-crown.

In these lines, the narrator realizes that war can be pretty awful. He knows that war is a kill-or-be-killed situation, and so he must shoot at and kill the foe he meets. However, he also understands that the only difference between his foe and himself is that they happen to be wearing different uniforms. He suspects that, were it not for the war, he and this man might become friends. They might go out for drinks together. One might lend the other money. Hardy's narrator has come to a mature understanding of what war really is.

In the excerpt from Stephen Crane's novel, Henry's mother has come to a similar understanding. She tells Henry that enlisting to fight in the Civil War is a "fool" thing to do. She knows the kind of person her son is, and she is concerned that he will do something foolishly heroic, that he will try to accomplish too much at once. So she warns him to be careful and not to let others influence him too easily. She seems more concerned about simple things like keeping warm than she is about any ideas of heroism.

Her son, Henry, feels differently. When he lies in bed and hears the church bell ringing to tell the news of some battle, he is excited and, despite his mother's warning, goes off to enlist. When he comes back in his uniform, he imagines a very dramatic farewell with his mom. He hopes that she will tell him to return "with his shield or on it," but she says nothing like that. Henry, unlike the narrator from Hardy's poem, has a very romantic attitude toward war. However, by the time he parts from his mother, he sees that his having enlisted causes her much pain.

Some characters in literature have a romantic attitude toward war. They think that war is exciting, filled with heroic possibilities. Others, usually older, more experienced characters, see war for what it really is. They know that war can be dangerous and deadly and that one might have to kill another person only because he wears a different uniform.

Commentary. The writer has decided that the body section of the essay requires three paragraphs, one for each of the three important characters. The writer has chosen to use four lines—an entire stanza, in this case—that express a complete idea. Notice how each paragraph contains a topic sentence, one that directly addresses the question ("how [the lines from the poem] apply to the scene"). Notice how effectively the writer has "proved" his points with appropriate details and explanation. In fact, the last body paragraph includes some directly quoted material.

COMPARE AND/OR CONTRAST

Consider this extended-response question:

Henry Fielding in *The Red Badge of Courage* and Marty in "Staying Home" have certain expectations of what it will be like to go to war. Describe their expectations toward war, and explain how their expectations are similar or different.

In your answer, be sure to include:

- descriptions of both men's expectations about war
- feelings or ideas that both men share, or feelings or ideas that reveal their differences
- details from both articles to support your answer

 Check your writing for correct spelling, grammar, and punctuation.

You probably have a lot to say in response to this question. The best way to proceed is to think about the different bulleted items. You know you're going to have to discuss both men's expectations about going to war, and you know that you'll need details from both pieces to support your answer. That leaves a couple of questions: Will you focus on similarities or differences, and how will you organize the response? Remember that organization is a flexible concept: You want to choose a structure that fits your purpose. With that in mind, examine this sample essay:

What does a person think about before he or she goes off to battle? What kind of outcome does a person expect? Henry Fielding in *The Red Badge of Courage* and Marty in "Staying Home" hope for positive outcomes, but their expectations are probably unrealistic.

When Henry breaks the news to his mother that he has enlisted in the Civil War, he is looking forward to hearing from her a certain speech. He thinks she's going to say something about "returning with his shield or on it." He has prepared himself for a "beautiful scene," and he has thought a lot about what he and his mother might say to each other. But his mother's words let him know that his ideas about heroism are a bunch of nonsense. She's more concerned about his staying warm and keeping quiet and not doing anything reckless. The tears she sheds upon his departure let Henry know that young men die at war, and she's concerned this might happen to him.

Marty hoped that enlisting in the Vietnam War would give him a much-needed sense of direction. He had been floundering in high school, and college didn't feel like an attractive option. Maybe four years in the Army would give him a chance to "find himself." That's not the way it worked out, though. Being in Vietnam was an absolute horror for Marty. He was exposed to death, suffering, darkness, and fear. He was so shaken by his experiences that he could not keep his hand still.

Both men expected that going to war would produce positive changes in their lives. Henry thought war would give him a chance to become a hero. Marty believed that war would give his life the direction it needed. Both men held unrealistic, naive expectations. Henry's mother tried to convince him of this, and Marty's experiences succeeded in doing so.

Commentary. This extended response uses a simple, direct structure to discuss a similarity between Marty's and Henry's expectations about going to war. The introduction begins with a pair of questions that serve to rephrase the question. The topic sentence provides the essay's main idea. The first body paragraph discusses Henry's romantic ideas about going off to war, using ample details from the passage to support the point. The second body paragraph discusses in detail the difference between Marty's expectations and the outcome. Finally, the conclusion ends the essay on a high note. It compares the two men's expectations and briefly mentions the feedback they received.

This particular question asks the reader to compare *or* contrast, but a question could ask for both.

TIPS FOR PARENTS

You may be thinking that this section is essentially a solo activity. However, you can help in supporting the skills involved:

1. Occasionally, you hear of teachers who encourage parents to read the same book that their children are reading. Quite often, parents end up thanking teachers profusely for this window into their children's literary lives.
2. Ask your children to make comparisons between cultural experiences. Does one TV show or film remind them of any other? In what ways are they similar or different?
3. Ask your children to share with you a favorite part of a TV show, a film, a book, a song . . . whatever. Children certainly know the lyrics of songs; maybe your child will be patient enough to explain them to you.
4. Once again, books on cassette are an excellent way to pass time on a long car trip and furnish a shared literary experience.

TIPS FOR TEACHERS

A few suggestions and guidelines to keep in mind:

1. Students need to be exposed to multiple genres so that they feel comfortable encountering the different genres this section will likely offer.
2. Students need to be reading from several works. Create opportunities to pair readings with similar themes, plots, styles, and so forth. Research projects (especially those of an interdisciplinary nature) provide an excellent opportunity for students to assimilate information from multiple sources.
3. Teach note taking and underlining. Make sure students know what it means to read actively.

4. Teach outlining. This essential critical thinking skill requires students to classify facts and concepts.
5. Permit students to organize their own work. Let them see that different organizational schemes will satisfy varying assignment requirements.

Once again, reading and writing are not the responsibility of the English Language Arts teacher alone! Familiarize your colleagues in other departments (school administrators, too!) with this section of the exam. Help them to see how these skills are essential to their subjects, too. Help them to develop appropriate activities. Work with them on developing interdisciplinary activities that will serve the skill and content needs of both disciplines.

ANOTHER SAMPLE READING-WRITING ACTIVITY

DIRECTIONS

In this part of the test, you are going to read an article and a poem. The article is called "Into the Forest" and was written by Michael Greenberg. The poem is called "Doors of Daring" by Henry Van Dyke. You will answer questions and write about what you have read. You may look back at the article and poem as often as you like.

Into the Forest

In 1941 German troops streamed across Poland, making their way into the very eastern recesses of that nation, into a region that is today the country of Belarus. These troops included the Einsatzgruppen, the feared Nazi killing units, and before long, the Jews of one small town, then another, were eliminated as a result of these Aktions.[1]

[1]**Aktions:** military actions

By the end of that year, the Germans had created a ghetto in the small town of Novogrudok. The Jews of the area were required to live there; among these were David and Beila Bielski, husband and wife, owners together of a small farm with a flour mill. In December of 1941, in a single day, the Nazis killed 4,000 people at Novogrudok, including the Bielskis.

Surviving this slaughter were the Bielskis' three oldest sons, Tuvia, Alexander, and Asael. The Bielski brothers, in their twenties, had lived their whole lives in the region and knew the cities, towns, and countryside like the backs of their hands. So, seeing the Nazi threat for what it was, knowing the Nazis would do their best to find and destroy them, too, they headed for the safety of the Nalibocka Forest, bringing with them a small number of survivors. Thus was born the Bielski Brigade. Their mission: to save as many Jews as possible.

Some Jews learned of this partisan[2] group known as the Bielski Brigade and attempted to locate—and join—them in the forest. Some succeeded; others, succumbing to starvation and the elements, failed. But the Bielskis also actively sought to increase their numbers, riding on horses through the forest, hoping to find ghetto escapees. They also visited the ghettos of nearby towns and tried to convince residents to attempt the risky escape. In fact, in this way, Alexander Bielski convinced his future wife, Sonia, to leave the ghetto; however, Sonia would not do so until Alexander promised to take her parents, too.

Gradually their numbers grew. Eventually the forest would be home to more than 1,200 Jews.

Surviving was a challenge, especially because Tuvia Bielski insisted that they accept all Jews—not just armed young men, as was the

[2]**partisans:** irregular troops engaged in fighting a powerful enemy

policy of other partisan groups. However, because the group was so diverse, a forest settlement sprang up, one that depended upon the skills of all its members. The settlement included a school, a tannery, and a hospital; butchers, barbers, shoemakers, carpenters, tailors, and even a doctor all contributed their expertise. Religious services were conducted. Babies were born. The spirit of cooperation prevailed.

To feed this many people, the Bielskis had to steal from nearby farms, and they had to convince the farmers not to betray them to the Nazis; their threats were convincing enough. A typical meal, cooked in huge pots, consisted of soup and potatoes. The settlement had its own flour mill, too, and baked plenty of tasty bread. A few cows yielded enough milk for the young and the sick. The food was not elegant, but no one starved.

The Bielski Brigade, led by the three brothers, conducted its share of military operations. Skilled and brave guerrilla[3] warriors, they fought and killed Nazis, disrupted German rail shipments, and punished those locals who collaborated with the Nazis. The Germans put a price on Tuvia Bielski's head. Sometimes, facing a threat, the whole camp had to pick up and resettle elsewhere in the forest.

In 1945, the war ended, and the Bielski Brigade walked out of Nalibocka Forest. (Asael was killed in battle on one of the last days of the war.) The survivors left Europe. Many came to the United States, including Tuvia and Alexander, who settled in Brooklyn, New York, and raised families.

Thanks to an unusual combination of bravery, resourcefulness, and humanity, more than a thousand Jews survived the Holocaust. Today, two generations later, their children and their children's children number in the tens of thousands.

---

[3]**guerillas:** groups of irregular soldiers specializing in surprise attacks and maneuvers

1. Complete the chart in order to show what these acts reveal about the members of the Bielski Brigade.

Acts Performed by the Bielski Brigade	What These Acts Reveal About the Members of the Bielski Brigade
The Bielski brothers actively sought to increase their numbers	
The whole camp had to pick up and resettle elsewhere in the forest	
They had to convince the farmers not to betray them to the Nazis	

2. In what ways was the Bielski Brigade different from other partisan groups? Use details from the article to support your answer.

_____

_____

_____

_____

_____

Doors of Daring
By Henry Van Dyke

The mountains that inclose the vale[1]
With walls of granite steep and high,
Invite the fearless foot to scale
Their stairway toward the sky.

The restless, deep, dividing sea
That flows and foams from shore to shore,
Calls to its sunburned chivalry,[2]
"Push out, set sail, explore!"

The bars of life at which we fret
That seem to prison and control,
Are but the doors of daring, set
Ajar[3] before the soul.

Say not, "Too poor," but freely give,
Sigh not, "Too weak," but boldly try,
You never can begin to live
Until you dare to die.

3. What do you think is the poet's purpose in writing the poem? Use details from the poem to support your answer.

_____

_____

_____

_____

_____

_____

[1]**vale:** valley
[2]**chivalry:** courageous persons
[3]**ajar:** open

PLANNING PAGE

You may PLAN your writing for question 4 here if you wish, but do NOT write your final answer on this page. Your writing on this Planning Page will NOT count toward your final score. Write your final answer beginning on the next page.

4. Choose a line or lines from Henry Van Dyke's poem, "Doors of Daring." Discuss the meaning of these lines, and explain how they apply to the article "Into the Forest." Use ideas from both the poem and "Into the Forest" in your answer.

In your answer be sure to include

■ the line or lines you have selected from the poem
■ an explanation of how this selection applies to "Into the Forest"

Check your writing for correct spelling, grammar, and punctuation.

_____

_____

_____

_____

_____

_____

_____

_____

_____

_____

_____

_____

_____

_____

_____

_____

Chapter 4

Writing Well and Effectively

 "Does spelling count?" Well, this is an English Language Arts exam, so of course it does! (However, you certainly know by now that there is a lot more to being a top-notch English student than spelling alone.)

Your work on the last two sections of this exam will be evaluated according to rubrics (see the Appendix). In case you are not already familiar with these, rubrics give teachers and students a clear sense of the criteria upon which students' work will be judged. Using rubrics tells students exactly what constitutes superior work, good work, and work that needs improvement. This way, there are no surprises. Understanding why you received a particular grade is easy.

For the Listening-Writing and Reading-Writing sections, your work will be evaluated according to these criteria: meaning, development, organization, language use, and conventions. (Note that only those sections accompanied by the spelling, grammar, and punctuation icon will be scored for conventions; the short-answer questions will not.) Improving language use and conventions skills is the focus of this chapter.

AUDIENCE AND PURPOSE

The ELA exam defines *language use* this way: "the extent to which the response reveals an awareness of audience and purpose through effective use of words, sentence structure, and sentence variety." Think of it as follows. Say you are interested—big time—in basketball. Over the years you have managed to accumulate a pretty impressive basketball memorabilia collection. And let's say you've been asked to deliver a brief talk about your favorite subject to two different groups. One is a group of 8th graders, the other 4th graders. How would these speeches differ?

Audience:	8th graders
Purpose:	to inform
What they need to know:	examples of dramatically profitable investments
	how to verify authenticity
	how to avoid questionable marketing firms
	the importance of keeping accurate records

Audience:	4th graders
Purpose:	to describe and entertain
What they need to know:	how I got started in sports memorabilia
	my first autograph
	meeting pro basketball players at card fairs
	my oldest basketball card

Your tasks on the ELA exam will require you to make similar distinctions. Before you write, think about these questions:

■ Why is my audience reading what I have written? Do they expect to be informed, entertained, or persuaded?

■ What does my audience want to know about the topic that I have chosen (or been assigned)? What vocabulary and language would be appropriate for these purposes?

What difference do audience and purpose make? Consider the example above. When you are talking with your 8th-grade audience, you will choose words and adopt a tone that will impress upon them the seriousness of your passion for collecting basketball memorabilia. On the other hand, when you are speaking to 4th graders, you will choose vocabulary that they will understand. You will adopt a tone that will convince them that collecting basketball memorabilia can be lots of fun.

On the Listening-Writing and Reading-Writing sections of the exam, your primary purpose is to demonstrate that you have understood the important ideas and details of the passages. Your composition's purpose, however, will differ according to the specific demands of that task. These are important distinctions to keep in mind as you write not only for the ELA exam but for other occasions, as well.

ORGANIZATION

You will be writing two extended responses (essays), one for the Listening-Writing section and another for the Reading-Writing section. When your essays are graded, the reader will care mostly about content—about how well you have understood the topic and the material and how thoroughly you have supported your ideas. But organization counts, too, because a well-organized piece is easy to read. It helps the reader follow your thinking and thereby understand what you have tried to say.

Do you remember the following extended-response task from Chapter 3?

Henry Fielding in *The Red Badge of Courage* and Marty in "Staying Home" have certain expectations of what it will be like to go to war. Describe their expectations toward war and explain how their expectations are similar or different.

In your answer, be sure to include:

- descriptions of both men's expectations about war
- feelings or ideas that both men share, or feelings or ideas that reveal their differences
- details from both articles to support your answer

Check your writing for correct spelling, grammar, and punctuation.

Let's apply these general principles of essay organization to this question:

■ A good introduction consists of two parts: a general statement and a thesis statement. The general statement shows that you have understood the question. You can construct a general statement in three ways. The paraphrase-contradictory-question (P-C-Q) formula will help you remember them.

1. You can **paraphrase** the question (*paraphrase* means to write in your own words). Here's an example: "Anyone going off to war would naturally wonder how the experience is going to turn out."

2. You can construct a **contradictory** statement. This means that you say the opposite of what you will eventually express. Here's an example: "Some people may think that going off to war is no big deal, but certainly someone who has enlisted would have to wonder what the experience will bring."

3. You can ask a **question** or two. Here's an example: "Have you ever wondered what it would be like to go off to war? Have you ever wondered how you would deal with that kind of challenge?"

Having composed the general statement, you will complete your introduction by writing a thesis statement. A thesis statement expresses the essay's main idea. When you write one, you will want to include the title(s), author(s), genres, and, of course, the main idea itself. Here's an example: "Henry Fielding in Stephen Crane's novel *The Red Badge of Courage* and Marty in Michael Greenberg's essay 'Staying Home' hope for positive outcomes, but their expectations are probably unrealistic."

■ Remember that the body of an essay is its heart. You want a good introduction to let your reader know where the essay is headed, but it's the body section that will get you the grade you deserve. So write a good topic sentence, one that provides more detail than the introduction's thesis statement. Here's an example: "Henry Fielding's naïve ideas about going off to fight in the Civil War come from romance novels, but his mother does her best to set him straight about what really matters in war, staying alive." You will want to follow this with pertinent details, material from the text that will prove and even illuminate your point. Should you quote material? It's not a bad idea, but for this task—and this test—you don't need to. Better to discuss details thoroughly and insightfully than to throw in a quote that adds little.

■ Conclusions sometimes befuddle middle school writers. They are not that difficult, but, yes, they do require some thought. Here are some options:

1. Highlight the key points of the essay. (Avoid verbatim repetition.)

2. Just as the introduction moves the reader from the general to the more specific, the conclusion can do the reverse: Discuss how your understanding of the passages might apply to life in general.

3. Connect this topic to another book you have read.

4. Sometimes you can use your conclusion to satisfy one of the bulleted items in the question. Do you remember the compare/contrast question in Chapter 3? The model answer uses the conclusion to compare the war experiences of the two men.

SENTENCE STRUCTURE AND VARIETY

Variety makes for interesting writing. If all of your sentences are as brief and as direct as the previous one, your writing will be choppy and dull. However, if you create a seemingly unending series of long, labyrinthine sentences, similar to the one you are presently reading, then your readers' eyes will soon grow too heavy to sustain the effort. Therefore, what you are looking for is an attractive mix.

Sentence variety can be achieved in three ways:

- Vary sentence beginnings.
- Vary sentence structure.
- Vary sentence length.

VARYING SENTENCE BEGINNINGS

Most sentences begin with subjects:

The *charismatic candidate* swept the election by an overwhelming margin. This *margin* was particularly great among women voters and college-educated voters. The *Republican Party* expressed its joy over the outcome and promised similar results in next November's national elections.

Each of these sentences begins with a subject: "The charismatic candidate," "This margin," and "The Republican Party." Notice what happens when we change just one sentence:

By an overwhelming margin, the *charismatic candidate* swept the election. This *margin* was particularly great among women voters and college-educated voters. The *Republican Party* expressed its joy over the outcome and promised similar results in next November's national elections.

Can you see how that simple change makes for a more interesting paragraph?

Here are some relatively easy strategies for varying sentence beginnings:

1. Begin the sentence with an adverb.

The batter *confidently* gripped his bat and waited for the next pitch.

Confidently, the batter gripped his bat and waited for the next pitch.

2. Begin the sentence with a prepositional phrase.

A plain old hot dog costs $5 *at the ballpark*.

At the ballpark, a plain old hot dog costs $5.

3. Begin the sentence with a transitional phrase or expression.

On the other hand, Jamel earned his highest grades in earth science.

For example, the price per share rose by 12 percent in January.

However, the Sunday train schedule differs considerably from those for the rest of the week.

4. Begin the sentence with a subordinate clause.

The program can be difficult to use *if you do not first read the manual*.

If you do not first read the manual, the program can be difficult to use.

Assessments have changed *because the State wants to hold students and schools to higher standards*.

Because the State wants to hold students and schools to higher standards, assessments have changed.

Each sentence in the following paragraph begins with a subject. Rewrite the paragraph. As you do so, try to change the beginnings of at least three sentences. You may, if you wish, add or delete words, but do not change the overall meaning.

People often underestimate the challenge of cooking even simple things. Take, for example, a basic pasta dish. Most cooks must resort to hard, packaged pasta, since fresh pasta is not available everywhere. Fresh pasta, in fact, is far superior, and no amount of sauce can camouflage the difference. Even boiling is not as simple as it sounds. Pasta must always be cooked al dente, firm to the touch, but many chefs are determined to overcook it to death! Pasta, for this reason, must be cooked through completely but only until it is firm. This invariably means boiling for less time than the pasta box directions will indicate.

_____

_____

_____

_____

_____

_____

_____

Now see how your paragraph compares with this one:

People often underestimate the challenge of cooking even simple things. For example, take a basic pasta dish. Since fresh pasta is not available everywhere, most cooks must resort to hard, packaged pasta. In fact, fresh pasta is far superior, and no amount of sauce can camouflage the difference. Even boiling is not as simple as it sounds. Always pasta must be cooked al dente, firm to the touch, but many chefs are determined to overcook it to death! For this reason, pasta must be cooked through completely but only until it is firm. Invariably, this means boiling for less time than the pasta box directions will indicate.

In order to emphasize a point, this model has changed the beginnings of six sentences. Changing fewer—or different sentence beginnings—would no doubt accomplish the same sense of varied sentence beginnings.

SENTENCE STRUCTURE AND VARIETY

The problem with grammar is that the terminology can be intimidating. In fact, a complicated-sounding term such as *predicate nominative* actually describes a rather simple, common linguistic event! That said, learning some terminology is essential to determining differences in sentence structure. For example, you will need to know the difference between an independent clause and a subordinate clause.

First of all, a clause is a group of words containing a subject and a predicate. Which of these is a clause?

1. Randi studies her vocabulary notes
2. When the wind howls
3. Which my sister gave to me
4. If you ever tire of Dickens's novels
5. Samantha accidentally spilled the test tube's contents
6. In the event of a blackout

Actually, the first five are clauses, as each contains a subject and predicate. Only the last is not a clause.

An independent clause is one that expresses a complete idea and can therefore be punctuated as a sentence.

Winston Churchill's courage and determination helped Great Britain survive the Nazi onslaught.

Is Derek Jeter the finest shortstop ever to wear the Yankee pinstripes?

Forty years after their heyday, you can still hear Beatles' tunes all over the airwaves.

A subordinate clause also contains a subject and predicate but does not express a complete thought and therefore cannot be punctuated as a sentence.

If you have never seen the Grand Canyon

Whenever you open the pages of a great novel

Because Peter copied his answers from Sylvie's paper

Which of the following are subordinate clauses, and which are independent?
1. Darryl barely passed the science exam.
2. Whenever the sky is this dark.
3. Which hardly ever happens.
4. My sister Sarah recently began working on Wall Street.
5. I just cannot seem to understand some of these formulas!
6. Because Samantha forgot to feed the dogs.
7. When you realize the advantages of using automated tellers.
8. The Mayor announced his plan to abolish this agency.

Numbers 1, 4, 5, and 8 are independent clauses. The others are subordinate and should not be punctuated as sentences.

With this knowledge under your belt, you are now ready for the four sentence types:

1. The simple sentence consists of a single independent clause.

Twice a week, *Janet completes a ten-mile run.*

The capital of Georgia is Athens.

In the beginning of the term, *Mr. Jenkins routinely forgot his students' names.*

2. The compound sentence consists of more than one independent clause, usually joined by a conjunction, but sometimes by a semicolon.

Allen Iverson can take anyone one-on-one, but *he still needs to pass the ball to his teammates.*

Yesterday I went to Jones Beach, and *I plan to return there today!*

Mrs. Smythe is one demanding teacher; she gives us homework every night.

3. The complex sentence consists of one independent clause and at least one subordinate clause.

If you ever travel to New Mexico, <u>be sure to visit Santa Fe</u>. (*Note:* The subject "you" is understood.)

<u>My sister,</u> *who lives in Portugal,* <u>will be spending the summer here in New York.</u>

<u>I failed the exam</u> *because I did not study.*

<u>Ricardo hopes to find a summer job,</u> *which should not be all that difficult.*

4. The compound-complex sentence contains at least one subordinate clause and more than one independent clause.

Omar forgot about our quarrel, but *I will always remember that he insulted me.*

When you begin your first year of high school, your new school will seem enormous, and you will miss your old middle school.

Cleveland's downtown area, which has recently experienced a rebirth, is well worth a visit, and the same can be said of Baltimore's Harbor District.

O.K., so now that you are the proud owner of all this grammatical expertise, to what use can you put it? Well, remember that the point of all this is variety. In your paragraphs and essays, you want to employ a variety of sentence structures. Once again, you are after an attractive mix.

One easy way to create longer sentences is by combining shorter ones.

A. Charlie smacked a line drive to right field. The ball was caught.
B. Charlie smacked a line drive to right field, but it was caught.

A. My friends and I often go to the Village. We also like to visit Soho.
B. My friends and I often go to the Village, and we also visit Soho.

In both cases, you have taken two simple sentences, and, by using a conjunction, created compound sentences.

You can also combine using subordinate clauses.

A. My sister prepared dinner. I set the table.
B. While my sister prepared dinner, I set the table.

A. The weather report calls for rain. I will take an umbrella.
B. Because the weather report calls for rain, I will take an umbrella.

A. South Dakota's weather runs to extremes. Its summers can be very hot, and its winters very cold.
B. South Dakota's weather, which runs to extremes, features very hot summers and very cold winters.

A. Paula's sister lives in St. Louis. The World Champion Rams play their home games there.
B. Paula's sister lives in St. Louis, where the World Champion Rams play their home games.

In each of these cases, you have taken two simple sentences and, by combining, created complex ones. By the way, you must surely have noticed that combining sentences varies not only sentence structure but also sentence length. In most cases, a simple sentence is shorter than other types. So, in a sense, you have killed two birds with one stone!

This awful paragraph sounds choppy because it contains too many short sentences (some of which are incorrectly punctuated as sentences). Try to address its deficiencies by combining some of the sentences to create more interesting ones.

One warning: Remember that you want to create a pleasing mix. Do not try too hard to combine all sentences into longer ones. If you do, chances are you will produce confusing, awkward sentences, which do not improve the writing at all. Look instead for natural combinations.

John LeCarre is a famous British writer of spy novels. His best-known character is George Smiley. In most ways, Smiley is a regular guy. He is short and pudgy. His marriage is falling apart. No one will ever mistake him for James Bond. A handsome, romantic spy. Smiley has some remarkable traits. First is his intellect. He possesses a brilliant mind. He uses his mind to see clues that others overlook. He uses his mind to reach conclusions that others cannot. Second is his determination. Smiley just keeps going after his goal. Even after he has suffered setbacks. Sometimes, he must decide to make personal sacrifices. He must do this in order to keep his goal in sight. For these reasons, Smiley eventually captures Karla. Karla is his Soviet counterpart.

_____

_____

_____

_____

_____

_____

_____

_____

_____

THE EFFECTIVE USE OF WORDS

You are not about to develop an astonishing vocabulary merely by reading this book. Vocabulary development takes years and results from repeated contact with all sorts of words. It has been said that you do not own a word until you have encountered it three times.

It is not the purpose of this text to provide you with a lengthy list of vocabulary words that you ought to master by test time. However, you should consider some useful strategies.

■ Keep a vocabulary notebook. One of those small phonebooks or even a 3-inch (7.5-cm) × 5-inch (12.5-cm) homework notebook, arranged in alphabetical order, will do the trick. (By the way, you can easily create a file on your computer for this purpose.) As you come across words you do not know, look them up, and enter them into your notebook. Over time, you will discover that you are looking up the same words more than once; in this fashion, you will gradually take ownership of them.

■ Do not use words whose meanings you are not sure of. Sometimes, using a difficult word correctly will impress. More often, however, using one incorrectly will stick out like that proverbial sore thumb.

■ Avoid slang. You need to be aware of your audience. Certain language is appropriate for exchanging notes with your friends or for writing e-mails and instant messages. However, the ELA exam is a formal writing occasion and requires you to use standard English.

■ Avoid overused words and expressions. Some students have a tendency to rely on words that are used so often and in so many ways that their meaning is practically extinguished. Some of these words are

nice	fun
really	great
a lot	sometimes

Some of these expressions are

She was *there for me*.

I awoke *bright and early*.

It was raining *cats and dogs*.

Look for these overused words and expressions in your own writing. Try to minimize them by finding appropriate, meaningful synonyms.

■ Good writing is in the verbs. Good writers develop a rich vocabulary of verbs because they know that a single apt verb can express so much. Consider these examples:

A. Jonathan goes to Sal's house after school.
B. Jonathan *frequents* Sal's house on a daily basis.

A. This summer, Jonathan will go to Venezuela.
B. This summer Jonathan will *journey* to Venezuela.

A. His teacher asked Jonathan to go to the blackboard.
B. His teacher asked Jonathan to *approach* the blackboard.

There is nothing wrong with the verb "to go," but you can see how each substitute expresses something else.

This paragraph includes some of the stylistic shortcomings addressed in this section. Some have been italicized, but you might locate others. See if you can improve upon them.

As a parent, I have mixed feelings about the sneakers that *kids* wear today. First of all, they are *so, so* expensive. *I mean*, they cost *mad bucks*. Some *go* for as much as $140. I know they might do much for your *hops*, but isn't that still way too much to pay? And there are *a lot* of different *kinds*, too. When I was a kid, we only had three kinds: Converse, Keds, and PF Flyers. Still, I have to admit that today's *sneaks* are *really nice*. With all those wild colors and *phat* styles, they are *really good looking*.

_____

_____

_____

_____

_____

_____

_____

SPELLING

Face it: At this point in your educational career, you are not about to become an outstanding speller overnight. But here's the good news: the ELA exam does not expect that to happen. The conventions rubric, even in its top level, does not insist upon perfect spelling. It does, however, look for a minimum of spelling errors, occurring primarily when students take risks by using sophisticated vocabulary.

With that in mind, you should focus on cutting down on your own spelling errors. One way to accomplish this goal is to keep an alphabetized list of your own spelling miscues. Most spelling mistakes recur, so you will have ample opportunity to note them. Teachers and peers will bring them to your attention, and so will most word-processing programs. If, for example, you have a tendency to substitute—incorrectly—*collage* for *college*, write the correct spelling in your notebook. Then, in the future, as you write and edit your work, you will have at your disposal a personalized checklist to help you correct these errors.

A second way is to become aware of common spelling errors. Here is a list of the correct spellings of 100 words:

accidentally	calendar	congratulations	doesn't
adolescence	career	conscience	eighth
a lot	ceiling	conscious	embarrass-
anticipation	cemetery	convenience	ment
appropriate	century	cooperate	enough
argument	certainly	courteous	environment
basically	character	criticism	exaggerate
beginning	chief	decision	February
believe	choice	definitely	forty
beneficial	college	desirable	government
bicycle	comfortable	disappoint	grammar
breathe	coming	disappearance	height
business	community	disease	heroes
cafeteria	competition	does	immediately

inconvenient	marriage	quiet	temperature
independence	mountain	quite	thorough
intelligence	necessary	realize	through
jealousy	neighbor	recommend	tomorrow
jewelry	occurred	responsible	tries
judgment	opportunity	ridiculous	usually
knowledge	persuade	says	villain
length	pleasant	schedule	weather
literature	possibility	separate	whether
loneliness	preferred	sincerely	
loose	principal	successful	
lose	principle	surprise	

As you can see, a number of these words require you to know simple rules involving common letter order (i-e or e-i) or the addition of prefixes and suffixes.

You also need to know how to make nouns possessive. The rules for this are relatively simple. Yet students confuse them surprisingly often:

Noun	Rule	Examples
Singular	add apostrophe and -s	Ralph's book a day's pay Paris's museums
Plural ending in -s	add an apostrophe	the students' lockers the nurses' uniforms
Plural not ending in -s	add apostrophe and -s	the children's bedroom the geese's feathers

Some students misspell contractions, usually by forgetting to add an apostrophe to show that letters have been left out. These are some common contractions:

I am . . . I'm
it is . . . it's
let us . . . let's
we are . . . we're
you will . . . you'll
were not . . . weren't

One last category of spelling error: the dreaded case of the homonym killers, whose wrath few students can elude!

Its/it's should be the easiest of the three. *Its* is a possessive pronoun: The lawn has lost *its* early spring vigor. *It's* is a contraction, a combination of *it* and *is*. If you can substitute *it is* for this homonym killer, then you know you are looking for *it's*, as in the following: We all know that *it's* important to start a new job on the right foot.

To/too/two should not pose as many problems as it does. *To* is a preposition: We strolled *to* the park. It is also part of an infinitive: We like *to* ski. *Two* always refers to the number: Today McGwire hit another *two* homers. *Too* is used in the sense of either *too much* or *too many*: She is *too* fast for me! It is also used as a substitute for *also*: I would like to go, *too*.

Their/there/they're is the worst of the three offenders. *They're* has a relatively narrow meaning—it is a contraction for *they are*—so you can use the same sort of substitution rule that you use for *it's*: *They're* going to the movies. *Their* is a possessive pronoun, and so its meaning is narrow, too: So many kids forgot *their* permission slips. That brings us to *there*, which has two very common meanings. The first is the *there is* or *there are* construction: *There* are five boroughs in the City of New York. The second meaning, just as common, refers to a place: Please leave the newspaper right *there*.

The following paragraph contains ten spelling errors. See if you can find them—and spell them correctly.

I haven't traveled alot, but a few years ago, I found my way too Chicago for the first time, and let me tell you: their is a city that won't dissapoint. I visited Chicago during the summer, so the whether is similar to what youd find in New York City, but its not the climate that makes me reccommend the Windy City. Chicago has some of the finest museums in the world, incredible shopping, a great ballpark in Wrigley Field, and miles and miles of waterfront fun. Getting around is anything but inconveinent, as Chicagos' busses and subways are prompt and fast.

1. _____
2. _____
3. _____
4. _____
5. _____
6. _____
7. _____
8. _____
9. _____
10. _____

CAPITALIZATION

The rules are fairly straightforward, although sometimes they can get tricky. For the most part, you need to distinguish between common and proper nouns. A common noun is a general category of noun; a proper noun is a specific person, place, or thing. This chart should make that clear:

Common Noun	Proper Noun
town, city	Syosset, Buffalo
body of water	Hudson River, Lake Placid
streets	Fifth Avenue, Milkwood Lane, East 11th Street
highways	Interstate 295, Taconic State Parkway
countries	Mexico, Japan, Afghanistan
mountains	Catskill Mountains, Adirondack Mountains
buildings	Empire State Building, Eiffel Tower
institutions	Parkwood Middle School, Cornell University
religions	Christianity, Islam, Judaism
nationalities, races	American, Asian, Hispanic
languages	French, Russian, Latin, English
holidays	Labor Day, Passover, Election Day
special events	World Series, New York Film Festival

Some confusion arises, however, over certain cases. Note the following:

▪ Sometimes, proper nouns can be used as adjectives. They should still be capitalized.

The *French* painter Monet composed some astonishing scenes of winter.

The library houses its share of *African* art.

▪ Do not capitalize the names of school subjects unless you are referring to a language or a specific course (for example, one followed by a number).

My favorite subject is *social studies*.

I earned a 95 in *Chemistry 101*.

▪ Capitalize the title of a person if it comes before a name or if you are referring to a specific person in a high office.

I hope that *President Bush* will sign the bill.

Is this the church where *Reverend Jackson* preaches?

The *Secretary of Defense* will meet with other administration officials.

I hope to become a *rabbi* when I grow up.

▪ Capitalize the name of a school. However, do not capitalize a type of school.

I have heard that *high schools* assign more homework but permit greater freedom.

The cheerleaders at *North Adams High School* perform exquisite routines.

▪ Capitalize a word showing a family relationship when that word is used before or instead of a person's name.

Hint: if the family relationship word follows a possessive noun or pronoun, do not capitalize. (Be careful here! This is one of the most common capitalization errors.)

I just discovered that *Cousin Phillip* is coming for spring break!

Rachel called, "Please don't wash my sweater, *Mom*!"

Peter's *mother* and my *father* are co-coaches of our basketball squad.

My *grandfather* was born in Eastern Europe.

■ Capitalize the first word of a title as well as all important words.

One Hundred Years of Solitude

"Mother to Son"

West Side Story

The Tragedy of Macbeth

The following paragraph contains ten capitalization errors. See if you can find them—and capitalize them correctly.

Until I was thirteen years old, my favorite subject was Mathematics, but my first encounter with the famous british author Charles Dickens changed all that. When I was a Middle School student, i had to read his novel *Great expectations*. The novel is divided into three sections, but my favorite is the first. In this section the reader meets the main character, Pip. Pip is an orphan, growing up in a small town in england, raised by his sister, Mrs. Joe Gargery, and her Husband, Joe Gargery. Mrs. Joe is a cold, harsh woman who boasts that she has "brought Pip up by hand," but it is kindly Joe who becomes not only a Father to Pip, but a friend, too. The section's most famous scene involves an escaped Convict, whom Pip meets down by the River. Although Pip is terrified, he shows the convict much kindness, thereby establishing his true character.

1. _____   6. _____
2. _____   7. _____
3. _____   8. _____
4. _____   9. _____
5. _____   10. _____

USAGE

What follows is a small sampling of the usage errors that so often plague student writing. Take a few minutes to make yourself aware of them; usually, that's all it will take to remedy the problem.

1. *of* vs. *have*: There is no such combination as "could of" or "would of" or "should of." You are really thinking of the contractions "could've," "would've," and "should've." You need to write "could have" or "would have" or "should have."

2. *everyday* vs. *every day*: "Everyday" is an adjective used to describe someone or something. Sally rejected her *everyday* putter and instead selected a new one. "Every day" works as an adverb, usually modifying a verb. The football team has practice *every day*. Ms. Stanton parks her car too close to the intersection *every day*.

3. *eachother* vs. *each other*: There is no such word as "eachother." Instead always write it as two words.

4. *have went* vs. *have gone*: The expression "have went" is incorrect. The correct way to express this thought is by using the words "have gone."

5. *accept* vs. *except*: "Accept" means to take willingly. I *accept* your offer of a ride to the mall. "Except" can be a verb that means "to exclude," or it can be used as a conjunction meaning "but." All students *except* those who have a reasonable excuse must attend the rehearsal.

6. *can* vs. *may*: "Can" refers to ability. I *can* run a mile in less than 5 minutes. "May" refers to permission. *May* I go to the bathroom?

7. *I* vs. *me*: Lots of people have trouble with this one. You need to keep this in mind: "I" must be used as a subject, whereas "me" can never be part of the subject. My brother and *I* love to listen to the oldies. Our mother gave my brother and *me* a stack of old records. (Confusion often arises when the I/me pronoun is paired with another word, but there's a simple trick: Omit the other word and see which one sounds right. Consider this sentence: My teacher gave permission for Tom and I/me to miss the next quiz. Leave out "Tom," and then ask yourself which sounds better: *My teacher gave permission for I* or *My teacher gave permission for me?* "Me" wins!)

8. *good* vs. *well* (and *bad* vs. *badly*): "Good" and "bad" are always adjectives. They modify nouns and pronouns. "Well" and "badly" are adverbs. Instead of saying, "I did *good* (or *bad*) on my test," you need to say that you did *well* (or *badly*). Confusion arises when we use the word "feel." Do you feel *good* or *well*? Actually, either is acceptable. Do you feel *bad* or *badly* about Tim's accident? In this case, "bad" is the correct choice because it is modifying the subject, "you," and serves as an adjective. O.K., sometimes English is confusing.

9. Double negatives are to be avoided. "She *never* sees *none* of her camp friends" contains two negatives. Instead, write "She *never* sees *any* of her camp friends."

10. *affect* vs. *effect*: "Affect" is usually used as a verb, meaning to influence. Does the weather *affect* your mood? "Effect" is usually a noun, meaning "result." You all know the *effect* of too much sun on pale skin.

Each of the following sentences contains an underlined word or phrase. If it is used correctly, write a check in the space. If it is used incorrectly, supply the correct answer.

1. _____ Terry and <u>me</u> picked up some tickets to the concert.

2. _____ Robert shines his shoes <u>everyday</u>, whether they need it or not.

3. _____ A mature student will <u>accept</u> responsibility for his actions.

4. _____ Sarah knew she had played <u>good</u> in the season opener.

5. _____ I <u>can</u> use a mouse with either hand, but it feels more comfortable in my right hand.

6. _____ I <u>would of</u> purchased a suit, but the prices were ridiculous.

7. _____ My teacher <u>doesn't never</u> give us homework on the weekends.

8. _____ The weather conditions will certainly <u>effect</u> the outcome of the football game.

9. _____ The twins have always been generous toward <u>eachother</u>.

10. _____ We <u>would have went</u> into the city, but our parents wouldn't let us.

PUNCTUATION

Books have been written about the subject of punctuation. However, for your purposes—improving your writing and succeeding on the ELA exam—a little brushing up will do. This falls into two categories: using the comma and punctuating dialogue.

Here are a few of the most important rules to remember about commas. Commas indicate brief pauses between separate elements in a sentence.

■ Use commas to separate three or more words and phrases in a series.

French, Italian, and Spanish are Romance languages.

I plan to travel through Canada, take an adult education course, and get in shape for the marathon during the summer.

- Use commas to separate two or more adjectives preceding a noun.

  Consider this important, necessary reading strategy to improve comprehension.

- To separate independent clauses in compound sentences, use commas after coordinating conjunctions.

  You may take the test now, or you may wait until later.

  John Irving is a gifted, prolific writer, for he has written many books that have captured the public's imagination.

- Use commas to separate interrupters and introductory nouns of direct address.

  Yes, Albany is the capital of New York.

  Dad, what is for dinner?

  My teacher, who was actually born in Algeria, speaks French fluently.

  Shakespeare's tragic heroes and heroines, each flawed in his or her own particular way, typically reach some level of understanding by the end of the play.

- Use commas after introductory clauses.

  If you are hungry, please help yourself to some leftovers.

  Before we leave the house, make sure we have everything we need.

- Use commas to separate dates and addresses.

  The delegates to the Constitutional Convention signed the Constitution on September 17, 1787, in Philadelphia, Pennsylvania.

Rewrite the following paragraph, providing commas where needed.

My cousin Rebecca who lives in Ohio will be studying in London England this summer. She is planning on taking college courses in English literature history and Romance languages. Yes Rebecca only fifteen years old is a very talented student and she has always earned spectacular grades in school. After she finishes her studies this summer she will return for her senior year in high school. At that time she will take advanced placement courses in foreign language biology and English.

Students seem to have a lot of trouble punctuating dialogue. The ELA exam will give you several opportunities to use quotation marks (as will your own writing, no doubt), so you may as well master these few rules.

■ Use quotation marks to surround words directly spoken or written by someone.

"Has anyone in the class seen Dr. Gold?" Helen asked.

Hamlet says to Horatio, "Give me that man that is not passion's slave."

■ Do *not* use quotation marks if you are paraphrasing another's words.

My mother told me I had to study before basketball practice.

Mr. Fisher said there would be five word problems on the test.

■ When a quoted sentence is divided into two parts, the second part begins with a small letter. (Note comma usage in these cases.)

"He found out," answered Jack, "that the moon is covered by a layer of dust."

"I wish," my sister mused, "that our father were not ill."

■ However, if a quoted section consists of more than one sentence, remember to capitalize as you usually would.

"For seven summers we've vacationed on the East End," Sarah said. "First we'd rent rooms in motels and inns. Then last summer we finally purchased our own home."

■ Question marks and exclamation points are generally placed inside the quotes.

Pauline asked, "What is your interpretation of the poem?"

Mrs. Angstrom warned Peter, "One more outburst and I'll summon the dean!"

■ However, if the question mark or exclamation point is not part of the quoted material, then place it outside the quotation marks.

Have you ever read Poe's "The Tell-Tale Heart"?

Rewrite each sentence, providing quotation marks where necessary.

1. I don't think I'm feeling all that well, I said to my mother.

2. My mother replied, Are you sure that the prospect of Mr. Miller's Latin exam isn't making you sick?

_____

3. No, I answered, my throat happens to be killing me.

_____

4. In that case you should call Doctor Bonner, my mother suggested. She has office hours today.

_____

_____

_____

5. That's a splendid idea, I replied.

_____

6. This way, my mother countered, you just might be ready for the Latin test tomorrow.

_____

7. My mother always thinks I'm trying to get over.

_____

SENTENCE STRUCTURE ERRORS

This troublesome category of errors afflicts many students and can be difficult to address. So often in our contemporary world, we are bombarded with communications that pay little attention to rules pertaining to the printed word. The sound bite has replaced the complete thought. From television, films, radio, music, advertising, and the Internet, we receive messages that fail to convey a proper sense of sentence structure.

What is a sentence? The age-old definition suffices. A sentence is a group of words that contains at least one predicate and its subject and that expresses a complete thought.

SENTENCE FRAGMENTS

A sentence fragment is a group of words that falls short of either or both of the above criteria. It is a piece of a sentence incorrectly punctuated as a complete sentence. Note the following examples:

I couldn't locate the remote. Which has a way of disappearing under the couch cushions.

John asked Marilyn to meet him at the Pierre. Located on Fifth Avenue and 60th Street.

Because of Sarah's late evening she did not complete her science homework. And forgot to study for the health test, too!

I have long admired Bernie Williams. A player who made the most of his considerable skills.

With each passing year, the Duponts became less enchanted with their suburban neighborhood. As they began to look for a place in the city.

I decided to take up stamp collecting. After seeing the impressive collection of my friend Malik.

In each example above, the second half is not a sentence. In most cases, sentence fragment errors can be fixed very easily, merely by attaching the fragment to an adjacent sentence.

Ernest Hemingway had never gotten around to completing the novel. Even though he worked on it for many years.

Ernest Hemingway had never gotten around to completing the novel, even though he worked on it for many years.

RUN-ON SENTENCES

Just as a sentence fragment is a piece of a sentence incorrectly punctuated as a sentence, a run-on is more than one sentence incorrectly punctuated as one.

I have never been to an Opening Day at Yankee Stadium, at least I get to watch on television.

Bob Dylan wrote hundreds of folk-rock hits, he also performed before huge crowds.

For three years Suzanne attended South High, this year she has transferred to North High.

The mayor has taken a hard line on union contracts, some people say he's given up on the labor vote.

I'm traveling to Maine this summer, I'll certainly consume my share of lobsters.

Each example contains a run-on error. You cannot join two independent clauses with a comma. (Sometimes this error is referred to as a *comma splice*.)

Fixing run-ons is simple. You can go about it in several ways:

- Create two sentences.

  I have never been to an Opening Day at Yankee Stadium. At least I get to watch on television.

- Create a compound sentence, either by adding a conjunction or by using a semicolon.

  Bob Dylan wrote hundreds of folk-rock hits, and he also performed before huge crowds.

  For three years Suzanne attended South High; this year she has transferred to North.

- Create a complex sentence. To do so, you will need to make one of the clauses subordinate.

  Because the mayor has taken a hard line on union contracts, some people say he's given up on the labor vote.

When I'm traveling to Maine this summer, I'll certainly consume my share of lobsters.

Students sometimes think that certain words and phrases—such as *however*, *then*, *on the other hand*—can be used to join independent clauses, but that is not so. Using them in that manner will create run-on errors.

Incorrect: Billy throws with his right hand, however, he bats from the left side.

Correct: Billy throws with his right hand; however, he bats from the left side.

 The following paragraph contains seven sentence fragment and run-on errors. Please rewrite the paragraph in the space provided, correcting all sentence structure errors.

Wall Street has certainly seen its share of recessions and corrections, however, none of these can compare with the Great Depression. Which officially began on October 24, 1929. A day known as Black Thursday. For the next three market days, stock prices fell, finally, on Tuesday, stockholders panicked, selling a record 16,410,030 shares of stock. Thousands of people lost unbelievable sums of money. Business and banks had also bought many shares of stock, they also lost a great deal of money and had to go out of business. Furthermore, banks had loaned money to many people. Who now could not repay their loans. Also, many customers, needing funds and skeptical of banking, had to withdraw their accounts from banks, as a result more than 9,000 banks closed within a four-year period.

_____

_____

_____

_____

_____

_____

You have now brushed up on your ELA skills, acquired helpful strategies in succeeding on the Grade 8 ELA exam, and honed your writing mechanics. Pat yourself on the back, and go for a 4!

TIPS FOR TEACHERS

It is not the goal of this chapter to suggest an entire mechanics curriculum but merely to foster an awareness in students of several key principles.

1. Make sure your students read and write a lot. From a growing sense of literacy emerges sensitivity to and skill in language use and mechanics.

2. Audience and purpose matter. Try to provide varied writing opportunities for your students. Participating in contests, submitting to publications, writing letters, and delivering addresses will all foster an authentic sense of purpose and audience.

3. With every formal writing assignment, focus on vocabulary development. One easy way to do this is to have students indicate three word choice changes that they made in the revision stage. When a student tells you that, as a result of having used his or her computer's thesaurus, he or she has substituted *intermittently* for *sometimes*, you know the student's expressive vocabulary is truly growing.

4. Nowadays students think that employing their computer's spell-check feature is editing enough, but of course that is not so. Teach students how to edit, not only to catch mistakes but mostly to make improvements. Build editing time into your writing assignments, and require students to demonstrate that they have, in fact, edited their work.

5. Much of this material can be taught effectively through minilessons. However, there has to be follow-up, either a quiz or some chance to apply these skills in writing—or both!

6. For some students, minilessons alone just will not do it; they will require additional attention. That is where writing conferences come in. Fifteen or 20 minutes of one on one can bring home to a student an especially tricky concept. It is well worth the time.

TIPS FOR PARENTS

1. Correcting a child's substandard usage has yet to improve any parent-child relationship, so, for the most part, you are better off leaving this one to the pros! That is, of course, unless your child asks for your assistance.

2. Be aware that children have their own informal language, which they use in conversation with their friends and in writing notes, e-mails, and instant messages. This language is as much a part of their identity as are their clothing and hair styles. While such language is informal, you might err in mistaking it for incorrect.

3. However, do make sure that you provide for your child's use a quality dictionary and thesaurus, and if you own a computer, a state-of-the-art word-processing program.

Appendix

- English Language Arts Rubric Chart
- A Student-Friendly, All-Purpose Rubric

ENGLISH LANGUAGE ARTS RUBRIC CHART

Listening-Writing and Reading-Writing

Quality	5 Responses at this level:	4 Responses at this level:
Meaning: The extent to which the response exhibits understanding and interpretation of the task and text(s)	*Taken as a whole:* —fulfill the requirements of the tasks —address the theme or key elements of the text —show a thorough interpretation of the text —make some connections beyond the text	*Taken as a whole:* —fulfill some requirements of the tasks —address some key elements of the text —show a predominantly literal interpretation of the text —make some connections
Development: The extent to which ideas are elaborated using specific and relevant evidence from the text(s)	*Taken as a whole:* —develop ideas fully with thorough elaboration —make effective use of relevant and accurate examples from the text	*Taken as a whole:* —may be brief, with little elaboration, but are sufficiently developed to answer the questions —provide some examples and details from the text —may include minor inaccuracies
Organization: The extent to which the response exhibits direction, shape, and coherence	*The extended response:* —establishes and maintains a clear focus —shows a logical sequence of ideas through the use of appropriate transitions or other devices	*The extended response:* —is generally focused, though may include some irrelevant details —shows a clear attempt at organization
Language Use: The extent to which the response reveals an awareness of audience and purpose through effective use of words, sentence structure, and sentence variety	*The extended response:* —is fluent and easy to read, with a sense of engagement or voice —uses varied sentence structure and some above-grade-level vocabulary	*The extended response:* —is readable, with some sense of engagement or voice —primarily uses simple sentences and basic vocabulary

Score point 0 = The responses are completely incorrect, irrelevant, or incoherent.

3 Responses at this level:	2 Responses at this level:	1 Responses at this level:
Taken as a whole: —fulfill the requirements of the tasks —address the theme or key elements of the text —show a thorough interpretation of the text —make some connections beyond the text	*Taken as a whole:* —fulfill some requirements of the tasks —address basic elements of the text —show little evidence that the student understood more than parts of the text —make few connections	*Taken as a whole:* —fulfill very few requirements of the tasks —address few elements of the text —show little evidence that the student understood more than parts of the text —make little to no connections
Taken as a whole: —develop ideas fully with thorough elaboration —make effective use of relevant and accurate examples from the text	*Taken as a whole:* —provide very few text-based examples and details —may include some inaccurate details	*Taken as a whole:* —provide almost no text-based examples and details —may include inaccurate information
The extended response: —establishes and maintains a clear focus —shows a logical sequence of ideas through the use of appropriate transitions or other devices	*The extended response:* —may show an attempt to establish a focus —may include some irrelevant information —shows little attempt at organization	*The extended response:* —shows little attempt to establish a focus —may be repetitive, focusing on minor details or irrelevant information —shows little attempt at organization
The extended response: —is fluent and easy to read, with a sense of engagement or voice —uses varied sentence structure and some above-grade-level vocabulary	*The extended response:* —is readable, with little sense of engagement or voice —uses minimal vocabulary —may indicate fragmented thoughts	*The extended response:* —is difficult to read, with little or no sense of engagement or voice —uses minimal vocabulary —may indicate fragmented thoughts

Writing Mechanics

Quality	3 At this level:	2 At this level:	1 At this level:	0 At this level:
Conventions: The extent to which the response exhibits conventional spelling, punctuation, paragraphing, capitalization, grammar, and usage	The writing demonstrates control of the conventions of written English. There are few, if any, errors and none that interfere with comprehension. Grammar, syntax, capitalization, punctuation, and use of paragraphs are essentially correct. Any misspellings are trivial or repetitive; they occur primarily when a student takes risks with sophisticated vocabulary.	The writing demonstrates partial control of the conventions of written English. It contains errors that may interfere somewhat with readability but do not substantially interfere with comprehension. There may be some errors of grammar and syntax; however, capitalization, punctuation, and spelling of grade-level words and use of paragraphs are mostly correct.	The writing demonstrates minimal control of the conventions of written English. There may be errors of grammar, syntax, capitalization, punctuation, and spelling.	The writing demonstrates a lack of control of the conventions of written English. The errors make comprehension difficult; the writing may even be unintelligible.

A STUDENT-FRIENDLY, ALL-PURPOSE RUBRIC

Criteria	Distinguished	Accomplished	Learning	Beginning
Meaning	Work demonstrates sophisticated understanding of the topic through insightful, complex response.	Work demonstrates solid understanding of topic through meaningful, honest response.	Work demonstrates basic understanding of the topic through appropriate, but predictable response.	Work demonstrates minimal understanding of the topic through an inappropriate or superficial response.
Development	Topic sentences are comprehensive and complete. Full, lucid body paragraphs contain illuminating details and examples.	Topic sentences are comprehensive and complete. Complete, clear body paragraphs contain appropriate details and examples.	Topic sentences are present but are too general or narrow. Body paragraphs contain appropriate examples and details, but these are not developed adequately.	Topic sentences are missing or too weak. Body paragraphs are skimpy and contain few good examples and details. Body section may consist of only one paragraph.
Organization	First paragraph establishes focus, suggests organization for the whole work. Body section maintains a logical sequence of ideas. Conclusion leaves reader on high note.	First paragraph establishes focus. Body section maintains a logical sequence of ideas. Conclusion highlights main ideas.	First paragraph addresses the topic in a general way. Body section develops ideas but may contain irrelevant or unclear material. Conclusion repeats intro.	First paragraph does not establish focus. Body section does not develop ideas logically. Conclusion repeats intro or is missing.
Language Use	Uses colorful, vivid, descriptive words (including figurative language). Sentences are varied and complete.	Uses effective and descriptive words. Sentences are varied and complete.	Uses plain words accurately. Sentences are awkward or contain some fragment/run-on errors.	Uses words incorrectly and ineffectively. Sentences contain many run-on and fragment errors.
Conventions: spelling, grammar, punctuation, editing	Work contains no errors. It is ready for publication.	Work contains very few errors. The writer has edited carefully.	Work contains some errors but can generally be understood. There appears to have been some editing.	Work contains many errors, which make comprehension difficult. The work does not appear to have been edited.

Index

Practice Exams

Practice Exam One

The ELA Grade 8 exam is a timed test, administered in two sessions. The first session includes Parts 1 and 2, Reading Comprehension and Listening-Writing. Allow yourself 90 minutes for the first session: 45 minutes for the Reading Comprehension, and 45 minutes for the Listening-Writing. The time required to listen to the listening passages is not included in the 90 minutes. The second session includes Part 3, Reading-Writing. Allow yourself 60 minutes to complete this second session.

You will find the correct answers to the multiple-choice Reading Comprehension questions in the back of this book. In addition, you will find model answers to the extended-response questions in Parts 2 and 3. Use these, in conjunction with the test rubrics, to evaluate the quality of your answers.

(Note to Teachers: Practice exams and answers are on pages that can be cut along dotted lines for easy removal.)

PART 1

Reading Comprehension

Note: You have 45 minutes to complete Part 1.

GO ON ➜

Directions

In this story, "The Wager," two college students make a bet with each other and must live with the consequences. Read the passage. Then answer the multiple-choice questions that follow.

The Wager

Paul and Roberta sat in the student union, sipping coffee. Since they'd started going out four months ago, meeting this way had become part of their daily routine.

Roberta, a history major, told Paul she was worried about an upcoming exam in her American History class. She really wanted to get an A on the test.

"You don't study enough," Paul said.

GO ON →

"I know," she admitted, sipping her coffee.

Paul decided to challenge her. "You'll never get an A on that exam."

"That's a creepy thing to say," Roberta replied, but Paul would not back down.

"You won't," he said, "not the way you study."

"You want to bet?" Roberta offered. "If I don't get an A, I have to take you out for a lobster dinner, but if I do get an A, then you have to pay."

"It's a deal," Paul said, and he offered his hand, but Roberta withheld hers.

"There's one other condition," she continued, her large brown eyes buzzing with mischief. "You say I don't work hard enough. Well, how's this? The loser has to work for the money. I'd waitress, I guess."

"And me?"

"You could work a day at Manpower."

Paul did not like waking at 5:30 A.M., but he had been told that was the only way to get a decent job at Manpower. If he got there early enough, he might land some kind of office temp position, and he'd get paid without having to break a sweat.

The walls of the Manpower office were institutional powder blue.

Behind the desk sat a middle-aged man with a large brush mustache and a name tag that read, "Mr. Douglas." Mr. Douglas, with his high-pitched twang, asked every job applicant if he had ever worked for Manpower before. Paul hadn't, so he needed to complete a lengthy application form, which he then submitted. Paul sat in one of the fifty or so plastic chairs positioned in the waiting area.

Paul waited, as one by one the other workers, all older than he, were called for jobs. Mr. Douglas handed each some paperwork and brief directions, and then he was gone. Paul watched the clock turn from seven to eight. He sat with his arms folded across his chest. He wished he had brought something to read.

At 8:30, Mr. Douglas called his name and that of an older gentleman. He handed the two men their paperwork and said, "You fellas will be doing some outdoor work today. Nice day for it."

In the parking lot, Paul and his workmate found seats in the back of a crowded Ford van. Paul introduced himself and learned that the other man's name was Henry. During the ride to the work site, Henry told Paul not to expect much, since the Manpower people usually saved the worst jobs for newcomers.

Actually, the work looked simple. Paul and Henry were dropped by a

GO ON →

railroad yard, not far from the highway. A supervisor brought them to a single train car, its side doors pulled wide open. All Paul and Henry had to do was unload the bags of flour and place them onto an adjacent flatbed truck. Didn't look hard, Paul thought.

The midautumn sky was gray like iron, but the air was still warm, so the two men removed their coats and began to work. Paul climbed into the train car, grabbed a burlap bag by its seam, and tried to lift it, but the thing must have weighed a hundred pounds! He couldn't lift it. Henry could, but he was a much larger man than Paul, and Paul didn't know what to do. Then he figured he could drag the bag to the edge of the car, dismount, carry the bag to the flatbed, and complete the process in reverse. This strategy worked, but Paul could barely carry the bag. Carrying even one required every ounce of strength he possessed, and there were hundreds of bags of flour.

Paul thought maybe he would just quit and tell Roberta that he hadn't been able to keep his end of the bargain, but he knew he'd feel awful doing that, so he decided to persevere.

At four o'clock Paul and Henry pulled the last of the bags from the train car. By then the air had begun to cool. Paul and Henry sat on the edge of the flatbed, leaning their sweaty backs against the bags of flour. They talked about places they had been and whether the Yankees would find their way back to the World Series.

Back at his dormitory Paul took a hot shower and then called Roberta. He made reservations for two at the Lobster Spot.

At the restaurant Paul showed Roberta his forearms. They were swollen to twice their normal size, and the veins were thick and cordlike. He told her his back hurt even more; she could see that he couldn't get comfortable in his chair.

Roberta smiled. Knowing that dismantling a lobster can be pretty tough work, she offered to help him with his. Paul smiled back. He felt the money in his back pocket and figured he would let her tease him this once.

GO ON →

1. Why does Paul tell Roberta she won't earn an A on the upcoming exam?
   A. She has never earned high grades on college tests.
   B. He doesn't want her to have unrealistic hopes.
   C. Paul is a mean-spirited person who routinely insults even those he cares about.
   D. He hopes this challenge will provide the incentive she requires.

   1. _____

2. Why does Roberta suggest that Paul, if he loses the bet, work a day at Manpower?
   F. She knows that Paul is not overly fond of hard, physical labor.
   G. Manpower offers the highest salaries for temporary workers.
   H. Manpower is eager to employ bright college students.
   J. Manpower's work schedules will accommodate Paul's schedule of classes.

   2. _____

3. Which of the following describes Paul's mood in the waiting room?
   A. ambitious
   B. impatient
   C. industrious
   D. confused

   3. _____

4. At the work site, Paul thinks of quitting, but decides to persevere. Which of these words probably means about the same as *persevere*?
   F. contemplate
   G. discourage
   H. persist
   J. cease

   4. _____

5. The next time Roberta expresses concern about an upcoming exam, Paul would probably
   A. suggest that she cannot earn the highest grade
   B. offer her a similar wager
   C. remind her how hard she studied for the last exam
   D. offer to tutor her

   5. _____

6. Paul first realizes how difficult his job will be when
   F. he completes the lengthy application
   G. he is riding to the work site
   H. he sees the wide-open doors of the train car
   J. he actually attempts to lift a bag of flour

   6. _____

GO ON →

7. At the end of the story, Paul decides not to respond to Roberta's affectionate teasing. Which of the following probably accounts for his decision?

A. He is in so much physical pain that he hasn't the strength to argue.

B. He just might need some help working his way through an entire lobster dinner.

C. Paul likes to tease, too, so he is comfortable with this kind of give-and-take.

D. He is satisfied that they have both achieved their goals and therefore sees no harm in her little joke.

7. _____

8. Which of the following best describes the relationship between Paul and Henry?

F. Paul and Henry will probably become good friends.

G. They have little in common, except for the satisfaction of a job completed.

H. Henry resents the fact that Paul has had opportunities that he could never enjoy.

J. One day Paul will likely become Henry's supervisor.

8. _____

9. By the end of the story, Paul has probably learned that

A. Roberta is far more capable than he ever realized

B. he should not attempt to forge a career in manual labor

C. applying effort and determination to a challenging task can bring ample rewards

D. newcomers are often required to shoulder the most difficult tasks

9. _____

GO ON →

Directions

"Go West, young man." So the saying went, and many men, most in search of California gold, obeyed. This traditional poem describes the experience of more than one young man.

The Miner's Lament

Author unknown

When the gold fever raged I was doing very well,
With my friends all around, young and old;
'Twas a long time ago, and I bade them farewell,
And embarked for the land of gold.

line
5   'Twas a hard thing to part from those little ones so gay,
That were playing in the yard round the door,
And my wife sobbed aloud as I started away,
Saying, "Farewell, I'll see you no more!"

Now the little gold locket my wife used to wear
10   Seems to fade by disease every breath,
Once happy and gay, now the picture of despair,
And those little ones all paler than death.

I dreamed I was at home in the old orchard tread[1],
With those loved ones so gay, it did seem,
15 As I reached for the apples that hung o'er[2] my head,
Disappointed I woke from my dream.

Cold, wet, and hungry, I've slept on the ground,
When those visions of happiness came,
But sad and disheartened, awoke by the sound
20   Of the screech-owl that lit on my claim.[3]

I toiled night and day with the hope of gaining wealth,
Through the cold winter's rain with delight,
But, alas! Sad misfortune has ruined my health,
So, my fond friends at home, all, goodnight.

[1]**tread:** walkway   [2]**o'er:** over   [3]**claim:** property

GO ON →

10. What happened to the locket that the wife gave to her husband?

   F. It was stolen by a screech owl.

   G. Its photos have faded with time.

   H. The miner sold it to make ends meet.

   J. The miner lost it at work.

             10. _____

11. What is the rhyme scheme of the first stanza?

   A. aabb   **C.** abab

   B. aaba   **D.** abcb

             11. _____

12. Based on the poem's overall meaning, the word *lament*, found in the title, probably means

   F. expression of regret

   G. financial profit

   H. a long, difficult journey

   J. family

             12. _____

13. The poem's last two lines probably mean that

   A. the miner's health will prevent him from returning to work

   B. the miner has not made as much money as he had hoped

   C. the miner will die from his illness

   D. the miner will soon see his family again

             13. _____

14. Which of the following sayings best captures the theme of this poem?

   F. "All work and no play makes Johnny a dull boy."

   G. "Haste makes waste."

   H. "Early to bed, early to rise, makes one healthy, wealthy, and wise."

   J. "The grass is always greener on the other side of the hill."

             14. _____

15. What is the source of the miner's "delight" in line 22?

   A. His memories of his family and friends

   B. The winter weather

   C. The scenic landscape

   D. The wealth he has already acquired

             15. _____

16. Which of the following does *not* describe the miner's experience in the West?

   F. His dreams of his family back home are rudely interrupted.

   G. Instead of becoming wealthy, he is forced to sleep on the cold, wet ground.

   H. His health suffers.

   J. He has made good friends among the miners he has met.

             16. _____

GO ON →

Directions

Often during a job interview, a prospective employer will ask about references, and an applicant may produce a letter of recommendation completed by a former employer. This is such a letter. Read it carefully, and answer the questions that follow.

January 17, 2001

To Whom It May Concern,

Rafael Sampson has asked me to write this letter of recommendation, and it is my pleasure to do so.

This firm first opened its doors in 1996, and Raphael has been a part of it since the very beginning. He was only fourteen years old, seeking a part-time, after-school job. When I asked him what skills he possessed, he replied, "I don't know anything about the printing business, but I'm a hard worker, I get along with people, and I'm willing to learn." This, I believe, was an accurate assessment—except that today, four years later, he now knows a great deal about the printing business!

Rafael began by answering phones, making local deliveries, and picking up sandwiches and coffee from the local deli. Gradually, however, by looking over people's shoulders, by asking questions, by making himself available, he began to learn about the sophisticated computer design programs that have become the tools of today's trade. Eventually, he was given a few small accounts. Here and there, he made the inevitable mistakes, some small, some not so small, yet, rather than get defensive, he acknowledged his errors and learned from them.

Rafael's people skills have proved invaluable. He is a good listener; as such, he responds to and respects the wishes of his clients. Therefore, customers are satisfied. When customers are satisfied, they bring us more business, and I am satisfied indeed.

GO ON →

Now that Rafael is going off to college, it is quite likely that he will bring his impressive skills to another employer. It is our loss but another's gain.

Sincerely,

Peter Marks

President, Impressions, Inc.

---

17. According to the letter, Peter Marks probably believes that Rafael's most valuable skill is his

A. ability to satisfy his customers' wishes

B. willingness to learn

C. refusal to become easily frustrated

D. warm telephone personality

17. _____

18. Which of the following best completes this sequence of Rafael's experience at Impressions, Inc.?

Seeks a part-time position

↓

performs simple errands

↓

_____

↓

manages his own small accounts

F. learns from his own mistakes

G. completes his high school education

H. asks for letter of recommendation

J. learns about computer design programs

18. _____

19. Which of the following statements would Peter Marks probably believe to be *false*?

A. For a beginner, no job is too small.

B. Any mistakes on the job are simply unacceptable.

C. Listen to the customer's wishes instead of your own tastes.

D. Working with people is at least as important as working with computers.

19. _____

20. Which of the following does *not* describe Rafael's performance at Impressions, Inc.?

F. When applying for his first job, Rafael admitted that he knew very little about the printing business.

G. Rafael began as a part-time employee.

H. Rafael attempted to conceal his mistakes.

J. Rafael earned the confidence of his employer and his colleagues.

20. _____

GO ON →

Directions

James Covell is a financial planner and money manager for RBC Dane Rauscher. His job requires him to work closely with clients in helping them achieve their financial goals. These include retirement planning, funding for children's education, and caring for various insurance needs. Read this interview, and answer the questions that follow.

Question: When did you first realize you wanted to become a stockbroker?

James Covell: It was the winter of 1983, and what happened was I became very friendly with a guy who was already in this business. We were skiing together, and he explained his work to me. He was very successful, he was enjoying it, he was making a lot of money, and he felt I would be perfect for that kind of job.

Question: What kind of training did you have?

James Covell: I had to study intensively to pass a rigorous exam, the Series 7, also known as the stockbroker's exam, but I realized that the most important part of my job involves communication. In college, I majored in English, read many novels, and learned to write pretty well, and these communication skills have helped me a great deal in my career. They are probably the most important factor in the success I've achieved.

Question: What kinds of skills and abilities does your work require?

James Covell: I need to have excellent listening skills. I need to have much patience, and I need to have a strong ability to explain things and situations to people.

Question: What do you like best about your work?

James Covell: Two things come to mind immediately. Number one would be

GO ON →

meeting and developing close relationships with many different people from different backgrounds. For example, it's interesting to me that I deal with many immigrants, people who came from different cultures and became successful in the United States, and I find these people and their success stories to be very interesting. Number two is the compensation that I get, which is very rewarding and affords me and my family the luxury of being able to do many things I'd always wanted to do, like travel.

Question: What do you like least? What's the hardest part of your job?
James Covell: It's hard to take a day off. The demands of the job are rigorous and require that an attentive broker be there all the time. Just last week, for example, I took a rare day off to attend the Yankees' home opener. Well, it just so happens that the market was doing a nosedive that day and, needless to say, my clients were very concerned about that. It was very difficult for me to enjoy myself at the ballpark, knowing that many of my clients would have liked for me to be available at that moment to explain what was going on.

Question: If you had not been a stockbroker, what do you think you might have done?
James Covell: I went to college with the intention of becoming an English teacher. That was my original plan, and I felt strongly that that was something I would like to do, especially since I had actually completed my student teaching. If I were to stop being a stockbroker, I would spend most of my time working with young people in some way, perhaps as a teacher. I would like to work with people who could use a good role model.

Question: What advice would you give to a young person thinking about a career in the world of finance?
James Covell: Such a person needs to be dedicated and prepared to work very long days. I would let that person know that no one in the world of finance becomes successful without investing a tremendous amount of time and energy. In other words, it's not an easy career, and there are no shortcuts, but the rewards, both monetary and personal, can be immense.

GO ON →

21. Which of the following has *not* been a factor in James Covell's path to success?
   A. He has learned how to explain things patiently to his clients.
   B. He has had to work long hours.
   C. He has learned how to listen well.
   D. He studied finance in college.

21. _____

22. Why is it so hard for James Covell to miss a day of work?
   F. Every day he misses means less income for him and his family.
   G. His clients often depend upon him to explain what is happening with their investments.
   H. People can easily find him, even if he decides to spend an afternoon at the ballpark.
   J. His supervisors monitor his attendance very carefully.

22. _____

23. Which of the following probably explains Jim Covell's interest in working with immigrants?
   A. He has the opportunity to learn some of their language and customs.
   B. These people are still adjusting to life in a new country.
   C. These clients have overcome many obstacles to reach their present level of success.
   D. He earns more money working with immigrants.

23. _____

24. What would James Covell probably say to a young person interested in becoming a stockbroker?
   F. "Take as many business courses as you possibly can."
   G. "In this career you won't have to worry about dealing with stress."
   H. "The keys to success are hard work and effective communication."
   J. "Forget about the business world. Think instead of a career in which you can help people."

24. _____

GO ON →

25. Which of the following best describes James Covell's feelings about his earning potential?

   A. Money does not matter as much as the satisfaction of helping people meet their financial goals.

   B. Earning a good salary enables James and his family to enjoy some of life's luxuries.

   C. The salary is not as great as people might think since the government taxes so much of it.

   D. James had always wanted to be wealthy, and he now proudly enjoys the satisfaction of making a huge salary.

25. _____

26. An appropriate title for this article would be:

   F. "A Fortune on Wall Street"

   G. "I Could Have Been an English Teacher"

   H. "The Rewards of a Difficult Career"

   J. "Learning to Listen"

26. _____

GO ON →

PART 2

Listening

 Note: You will have 45 minutes to complete Part 2. This does not include the time it takes to listen to both passages twice.

GO ON →

Directions

In this part of the test, you will listen to two essays. (The essays appear on pages 202 to 205 at the end of the book. Have a friend or family member read them to you.) The first, written by Professor Gerald Early, is called "Learn or Burn." The second, written by Ava Hoffman, an 8th-grade student, is called "The Obstacle." Then you will answer some questions to show how well you understood what was read.

You will listen to the essays twice. As you listen to the essays, you may want to take notes. You may take notes at any time during the readings. You may use these notes to answer the questions that follow. Use the space below and on the next page for your notes.

Here are some words and definitions you will need to know as you listen to the essays.

"Learn or Burn"
- **tedious**   boring, tiring
- **aggrieved**   hurt, wounded
- **superficially** on the surface, outwardly
- **patronizing**   talking down to

"The Obstacle"
- **jubilant**   rejoicing, triumphant

NOTES

GO ON →

NOTES

GO ON →

27. Professor Early claims "there is a price to pay for being taken seriously." Explain what this sentence means, using information from "Learn or Burn."

_____

_____

_____

_____

_____

_____

28. In "Learn or Burn," the student claims that Professor Early hates students, but Professor Early insists that he respects them very much. What reasons do they give for their opinions? Use details from the passage.

Why the Student Believes Professor Early Hates Students	Why Professor Early Insists He Respects Students Very Much

29. According to Ava Hoffman, why is it a bad idea to stay mad at one's teacher? Use information from her essay in your answer.

_____

_____

_____

_____

_____

GO ON →

PLANNING PAGE

You may PLAN your writing for question 30 here if you wish, but do NOT write your final answer on this page. Your writing on this Planning Page will NOT count toward your final score. Write your final answer beginning on the next page.

GO ON →

30. Professor Gerald Early and 8th grader Ava Hoffman think about grades in very different ways. What would Professor Early learn from Ava Hoffman, and what would Ava Hoffman learn from Professor Early?

In your response, be sure to include

- ◼ what Professor Early would learn from Ava Hoffman about grades
- ◼ what Ava Hoffman would learn from Professor Early about grades
- ◼ details from both essays

✔ **Check your writing for spelling, grammar, and punctuation.**

_____

_____

_____

_____

_____

_____

_____

_____

_____

_____

_____

_____

_____

_____

_____

_____

_____

GO ON →

_____

_____

_____

_____

_____

_____

_____

_____

_____

_____

_____

_____

_____

_____

_____

_____

_____

_____

_____

_____

_____

_____

_____

STOP

PART 3

Reading

 Note: You will have 60 minutes to complete Part 3. You may not go back to Part 1 or Part 2.

GO ON →

Directions
In this part of the test, you will read an article and a poem. The article is called "My Father" and was written by Cheryl Behnam, a 13-year-old girl. The poem is called "Our Ancestors"; its author is unknown.

My Father

By Cheryl Behnam

My father, Rafael Behnam, had lived in Mashad, Iran, for all his life, but, after graduating from high school, his parents decided it would be best if he went to the United States to continue his education. His Uncle Pierre and Aunt Charlene lived in Chicago, Illinois, so it seemed like the optimal place for him to go. He would enroll in Roosevelt University, and everything would fall into place.

To my father, though, everything wasn't so perfect. The United States was another world to him, and he would be just one of the thousands of immigrants trying to make something of himself. How could he leave everything and every-

GO ON →

one he had ever known to pursue a life in America? In any case, my father did end up leaving Iran, armed with a suitcase and a carpet, to embark on a new life in the United States.

Arriving in the United States was a bizarre experience for my father. Chicago was unlike anything he had known, unlike anything he had expected. Iran was like a playground compared to Chicago's enormity and modernity. Homesickness hit him hard; he found himself yearning to see his family, friends, and old neighborhood again. Everything there had been familiar and comfortable; there he had never felt uneasy or out of place. He was not used to the American ways of life. Although his family members were extremely kind to him, their house didn't seem like his home, just a place of residence.

Another obstacle was my father's fear of not accomplishing his academic goals. After all, that was the reason he had ventured to America in the first place. His problems with the language troubled him to no end. His whole vernacular[1] was based around Farsi, the official language of Iran. He was also worried about finding friends in his classes and dormitory. With all their differences, how would they ever find common ground? Also, his parents were depending on him to fulfill all of his educational goals in America. If he failed, his parents would be disappointed in him. The pressure was getting to him.

That autumn, however, he realized he could no longer just complain about his problems. He had to find solutions to them. His ultimate goal was to become a doctor, and, as his lessons began he immediately became interested, and he saw that his ambition urged him to succeed. He began to meet his peers, and at last he had people his age to converse with about all of the things that were happening to him. His new friends taught him about their culture, and he did the same, and this connected them in a unique way. My father gradually became acquainted with the American ways, by eating the food, by enjoying the culture. A highlight of his day was watching "The Tonight Show with Johnny Carson" with his friends in the dorm. At first he had a hard time understanding the jokes, but he soon learned to appreciate them. As college life continued, he soon found his place in Chicago.

My father realized that every day brought him new opportunities. Obviously, things weren't exactly perfect, but they were definitely

[1]**vernacular:** everyday language

GO ON →

improving as time passed. He was adapting to the language and scholastic level of Roosevelt University. Becoming a physician remained his goal and provided for him an intense daily focus. Part of his growing comfort was definitely due to his friends and family. The dorm had become a support system for him, where he could share his interests and learn from others as well. As for his relatives, they had become a second family, making their house his home-away-from-home. When homesickness plagued him, being with his relatives and practicing their traditions—going to temple or eating a Persian meal—eased his transition. Plus, he got to experience the everyday excitement of living in an extensive city like Chicago, a place where remarkable things happen daily.

All of his hard work paid off. In February of 1976 my father graduated from Roosevelt University. He could now start his career and adult life. My father also commended himself on the fact that although he had grown as a person, he still kept the old traditions that his parents had taught him. He had let America influence him, but he did not change his beliefs. He appreciated his heritage and intended not only to continue practicing his traditions but to teach them to his own family as it grew. To his parents this meant more than all the diplomas in the world.

GO ON →

31. Complete the chart with words or phrases that describe Rafael Behnam's character. Identify information from the essay that supports each character trait.

Character Trait	Supporting Information

32. Cheryl Behnam writes of her father, "He had let America influence him, but he did not change his beliefs."

Explain what this sentence means, using details from the essay.

_____

_____

_____

_____

_____

_____

_____

GO ON →

Our Ancestors

Author unknown

If you could see your ancestors
All standing in a row
Would you be proud of them or not
Or don't you really know?

Some strange discoveries are made
In climbing family trees
And some of them, you know,
Do not particularly please.

If you could see your ancestors
All standing in a row,
There might be some of them perhaps
You wouldn't care to know.

But there's another question, which
Requires a different view:
If you could meet your ancestors,
Would they be proud of you?

---

33. The last stanza of the poem discusses a "different view." What is this view, and how is it different from the ideas expressed in the rest of the poem? Use information from the poem in your answer.

_____

_____

_____

_____

_____

_____

GO ON →

PLANNING PAGE

You may PLAN your writing for question 34 here if you wish, but do NOT write your final answer on this page. Your writing on this Planning Page will NOT count toward your final score. Write your final answer on the following pages.

GO ON →

34. Choose a line or lines from the poem "Our Ancestors." Discuss the meaning of your selection, and explain how it does *or* does not apply to Cheryl Behnam's essay about her father. Use ideas from BOTH the poem and the essay in your answer.

In your answer, be sure to include

- the line or lines you have selected from the poem
- an explanation of what those lines mean
- an explanation of how those lines apply *or* do not apply to what Cheryl Behnam learned about her father

✔ **Check your writing for correct spelling, grammar, and punctuation.**

_____

_____

_____

_____

_____

_____

_____

_____

_____

_____

_____

_____

_____

_____

_____

GO ON →

STOP

Answers to Practice Exam One

ANSWERS TO PART 1: READING COMPREHENSION

1. D	7. D	13. C	19. B	25. A
2. F	8. G	14. J	20. H	26. H
3. B	9. C	15. A	21. D	
4. H	10. G	16. J	22. G	
5. C	11. C	17. A	23. C	
6. J	12. E	18. J	24. H	

ANSWER TO PART 2: LISTENING

LISTENING PASSAGES

Learn or Burn

By Professor Gerald Early

I, like most of my colleagues, hate to grade papers. It is tedious and mentally exhausting. I spend hours grading papers, going through them with a fine-tooth comb. Some students are a bit shaken when they get their papers back covered in a sea of red ink. But despite the appearance of the paper, I am a very gentle soul, and I almost always give a student as high a grade as I can reasonably justify and responsibly offer. It usually turns out to be the same grade the student would have earned taking the same subject matter with any other professor. I remember one young woman came to my office, very upset with how I graded her paper. She said I was too harsh a grader, that I must hate students because I was so hard on her paper. And on and on she went, aggrieved and demanding a grade change.

I said to her, "I graded your paper fairly. As you can tell, I read it very carefully. Now, the problem here is that you are disturbed that I took more care and time grading your paper than you did writing it. You shouldn't be disturbed by that. That is to be expected. Far from hating students, I have the highest respect for them. And I show that respect by the way I grade your papers, by the time I put into it. I take what you say seriously. That is why I so thoroughly graded your paper. Now, I could read your paper very superficially, attach some [routine] remarks and give you a gentleman's B. But if I did that I would not be taking you or your work seriously. I would be dismissing you as someone not really worthy of my time and training. I would then be patronizing you. Then, whether you know it or not, you would lose all respect for me. I would be worthless to

GO ON ➔

you as a teacher. Is that what you want? The choice is yours. What would you prefer?"

She blushed a bit, held her head down, obviously embarrassed, and was silent for some time.

"I want to be taken seriously," she said finally.

"So do we all," I said. "So do we all. But there is a price to pay for being taken seriously. And the standards are high. Emerson once said, 'People do not deserve to have good writing, they are so pleased with bad.' So now you know that even the best-intentioned criticism hurts. Good. Don't stand around being hurt and expecting that temper tantrums will get me to change your grade. Read what I have written on your paper, take it to heart, and practice writing. Learn or burn, as my mother used to tell me, learn or burn."

The Obstacle

By Ava Hoffman

The time between the point at which your teacher announces that she has corrected the tests and will hand them out and the point at which you have it in your hand is excruciating. That anxious, nervous feeling inside of you tells you how well you think you did.

There are many kinds of reactions you can have. The first, the most painful category, is the failing grade one. Two branch off of this: the solo failure or the group failure. With the group failure, you can easily say that the teacher should have taught more, because it is evident that the class did not learn the subject well. The solo failure signifies that you need to study more.

Then you have the jubilant high score test. Either way, whether you are the only one in the class that scored so well, or if everyone in the class did great, you are happy. Something falls in the middle of these, and the reaction can be good or bad, depending how you feel that day. I guess I didn't feel too great the day I got my grade. It wasn't even that I had failed, because I hadn't. It was more that I was just mad, because I shouldn't have gotten that grade. Some people will say, "Oh, don't worry about it. You'll do better on the next test." Well, whether or not I do well on the next test is not the point. The point is that I want a better grade on the test I just took.

When I got my test back from my teacher, I walked right out of the classroom. Luckily, Mrs. Perkins decided to give them out at the last minute of the period. With her fake smile, she always says, "Have a good day" to people as they walk out of the door. Well, I didn't want to have to deal with the "you, too" response, so I just left.

I knew that I didn't deserve the grade that I had got. Since it wasn't the type of test that had answers that were either right or wrong, I couldn't exactly argue. I knew that it wasn't an argument I could win, in the sense that even if I won it, the teacher wouldn't forget, and I'd lose out in the long run.

The worst part about it all, though, is that you can't stay mad at your teacher. If you're mad, you don't want to join in the discussions, and you don't want to answer questions that you know when no one else does. If you do this, you won't get a class participation grade, and you won't feel the pride that you get from answering a hard question. The whole situation is rather frustrating. So you just leave it alone, and try to do as well as you can on the next test.

Teachers think that if a student gets a bad grade, it's the student's fault. Maybe teachers should take a closer look at this, because I'm sure their recollection of receiving bad grades is close to nonexistent. It doesn't matter if the teacher is older or right out of school. Once you cross over into the world of the teacher, you won't understand as well what it feels like to be the student.

The next time you get a bad grade—and most of us will get a bad grade again—just think back to this. Just the satisfaction of knowing you are not alone should make you smile.

---

30. Professor Gerald Early and 8th grader Ava Hoffman think about grades in very different ways. What would Professor Early learn from Ava Hoffman, and what would Ava Hoffman learn from Professor Early?

In your response, be sure to include

- what Professor Early would learn from Ava Hoffman about grades
- what Ava Hoffman would learn from Professor Early about grades
- details from both essays

 Check your writing for correct spelling, grammar, and punctuation.

Students and teachers think about grades in different ways. For that reason, if eighth grader Ava Hoffman and Professor Gerald Early sat down to discuss the matter, they would probably learn a great deal from each other.

Ava would probably learn that teachers care just as much about grades as students do. Even though grading papers is very hard work, teachers like Professor Early put in the time needed to do the job well. That is because they take their students' work very seriously. In his speech, Professor Early discusses the time a student came to his office to complain about a grade. She accused him of being a very harsh grader. However, Professor Early explained that he had worked very hard on her paper because he believes it is important to take students' work seriously. He could have given her a gentleman's B, but that would be patronizing her. Professor Early explained to the young lady that the price for being taken seriously is that the standards are then high, and so plenty of criticism will be coming her way. Students need to deal with that criticism, Professor Early says, if they really want to learn.

Professor Early would probably learn from Ava Hoffman that many students are very serious about their work, but they do not feel as if they can discuss their work with teachers. Students like Ava take their test results very personally and can become very upset if they score lower than they had expected. Sometimes students feel they do not deserve a particular grade but that talking to the teacher would be pointless. Even if the student won the argument, the teacher might hold a grudge, and so the student would lose out in the long run. Ava also believes that too many teachers forget what it is like to be a student. Teachers automatically assume that a bad grade is the student's fault, but it just could be that the teacher has not taught the material well enough. In any case, Ava claims, teachers are not willing to admit to this.

Students and teachers may bring different points of view to the subject of tests and grades, but it is very important that each hears what the other party thinks about the subject. If teachers and students can communicate about this subject, maybe they can reduce the misunderstandings that have existed for a long time.

ANSWER TO PART 3: READING

34. Choose a line or lines from the poem "Our Ancestors." Discuss the meaning of your selection, and explain how it applies to Cheryl Behnam's essay about her father. Use ideas from BOTH the poem and the essay in your answer.

In your answer, be sure to include

- the line or lines you have selected from the poem
- an explanation of what those lines mean
- an explanation of how those lines apply to what Cheryl Behnam learned about her father

 Check your writing for correct spelling, grammar, and punctuation.

The poem "Our Ancestors" includes these lines: "If you could see your ancestors/ All standing in a row/ Would you be proud of them or not/ Or don't you really know?" These lines tell us that sometimes we do not have enough information about our ancestors to know how we actually feel about them.

Because of a school assignment, Cheryl Behnam had to interview her father. As a result, she learned information that made her very proud of him.

Cheryl learned that her father, Rafael, had to overcome many obstacles when he first came to America from Iran. Adjusting to life in Chicago was very difficult. Of course he was homesick, and of course Chicago seemed huge and modern, compared with Iran. What worried him most, though, were the academic and social adjustments he would have to make. After all, his family was depending upon him to succeed in his desire to become a physician. Despite some setbacks, Rafael found his way. He gradually learned the language, made friends in school, and performed well in his classes. Finally in 1976 he graduated from Roosevelt University! By hearing this story, Cheryl must have learned that her father was a determined, hardworking, and resourceful man.

Cheryl also probably learned that culture and tradition mattered very much to her father. When he first came to America, Rafael did not want to lose all his Iranian ways. He was concerned that as he mastered the ways of his new country, he might give up the ways of his old, but that did not happen. Fortunately, he had in Chicago a home away from home. His Uncle Pierre and Aunt Charlene lived there, and therefore Rafael could spend time with them, eating Persian meals, going to temple, practicing his traditions, which meant a lot to him. In fact, even though he adjusted successfully to America, he was determined not only to keep his traditions but also to teach them to his own family, once he had one. To his parents this was an accomplishment equal to his academic ones.

Because of a school assignment, Cheryl Behnam learned things about her father she probably would not have known. As a result, if she saw her "ancestors all standing in a row," she could easily pick him out—as a man she definitely admires.

Practice Exam Two

The ELA Grade 8 exam is a timed test, administered in two sessions. The first session includes Parts 1 and 2, Reading Comprehension and Listening-Writing. Allow yourself 90 minutes for the first session, 45 minutes for the Reading Comprehension, and another 45 minutes for the Listening-Writing. The time required to listen to the listening passages is not included in the 90 minutes. The second session includes Part 3, Reading-Writing. Allow yourself 60 minutes to complete this second session.

You will find the correct answers to the multiple-choice reading comprehension questions in the back of this book. In addition, you will find model answers to the extended-response questions in Parts 2 and 3. Use these, in conjunction with the test rubrics, to evaluate the quality of your answers.

(Note to Teachers: Practice exams and answers are on pages that can be cut along dotted lines for easy removal.)

Reading Comprehension

Note: You will have 45 minutes to complete Part I.

GO ON ➔

Directions

Read this excerpt from the short story "The Egg" by Sherwood Andersen. Then answer the multiple-choice questions that follow.

The Egg

My father was, I am sure, intended by nature to be a cheerful, kindly man. Until he was thirty-four years old he worked as a farm hand for a man named Thomas Butterworth whose place lay near the town of Bidwell, Ohio. He had then a horse of his own and on Saturday evenings drove into town to spend a few hours in social intercourse[1] with other farm hands. In town he drank several glasses of beer and stood about in Ben Head's saloon—crowded on Saturday evenings with visiting farm hands. Songs were sung and glasses thumped on the bar. At ten o'clock father drove home along a lonely country road, made his horse comfortable for the night and himself went to bed, quite happy in his position in life. He had at that time no notion of trying to rise in the world.

It was in the spring of his thirty-fifth year that father married my mother, then a country school teacher, and in the following spring I came wriggling and crying into the world. Something happened to the two people. They became ambitious. The American passion for getting up in the world took possession of them.

It may have been that mother was responsible. Being a school teacher she had no doubt read books and magazines. She had, I presume, read of how Garfield, Lincoln, and other Americans rose from poverty to fame and greatness and as I lay beside her—in the days of her lying-in—she may have dreamed that I would some day rule men and cities. At any rate she induced father to give up his place as a farm hand, sell his horse and embark on an independent enterprise of his own. She was a tall silent woman with a long nose and troubled gray eyes. For herself she wanted nothing. For father and myself she was incurably ambitious.

[1]**intercourse:** interaction

GO ON →

The first venture into which the two people went turned out badly. They rented ten acres of poor stony land on Grigg's Road, eight miles from Bidwell, and launched into chicken raising. I grew into boyhood on the place and got my first impressions of life there. From the beginning they were impressions of disaster and if, in my turn, I am a gloomy man inclined to see the darker side of life, I attribute it to the fact that what should have been for me the happy joyous days of childhood were spent on a chicken farm.

1. The reader can assume that the narrator is:
   A. a child living in the country
   B. a child who has moved to the city
   C. an adult looking back on his childhood
   D. a teacher

   1. _____

2. The narrator's father enjoyed his life as a farm hand because:
   F. he enjoyed the simple pleasures of country life
   G. he knew that his life was about to change
   H. he enjoyed the companionship of other farm laborers
   J. he did not require a great deal of money

   2. _____

3. To the narrator President Lincoln is an example of someone who:
   A. was dedicated to the principle of equality
   B. traveled a path from poverty to greatness
   C. was very different from his father
   D. benefited from having an ambitious wife

   3. _____

4. The narrator resembles his father in that both men:
   F. became gloomy adults
   G. eventually became successful farmers
   H. married ambitious women
   J. were satisfied with their lives

   4. _____

GO ON →

5. The narrator says of his mother, "At any rate she induced father to give up his place as a farm hand." *Induced* most nearly means:
   A. persuaded
   B. flattered
   C. forced
   D. desired

5. _____

6. Which statement would contradict the narrator's claim that his mother was responsible for his father's ambition?
   F. His mother always wanted the best for her husband and child.
   G. His mother did not become ambitious until her first child was born.
   H. After the chicken farm failed, his father became a successful rancher.
   J. His father had always wanted a farm of his own.

6. _____

7. According to the last paragraph, which of the following is definitely *not* responsible for the change in the narrator's character?
   A. the poor quality of the land
   B. his own ambitions
   C. the nature of chicken farming
   D. the fact that the business failed

7. _____

GO ON →

Directions

Read the poem "The Daffodils" and answer the questions that follow.

The Daffodils
By William Wordsworth

I wander'd lonely as a cloud
That floats on high o'er vales and hills,
When all at once I saw a crowd,
A host of golden daffodils,
line 5   Beside the lake, beneath the trees,
Fluttering and dancing in the breeze.

Continuous as the stars that shine
And twinkle on the Milky Way,
They stretch'd in never-ending line
10   Along the margin of a bay:
Ten thousand saw I at a glance
Tossing their heads in sprightly[1] dance.

The waves beside them danced, but they
Out-did the sparkling waves in glee:—
15   A Poet could not but be gay[2]
In such a jocund[3] company!
I gazed—and gazed—but little thought
What wealth the show to me had brought;

For oft, when on my couch I lie
20   In vacant or in pensive mood,
They flash upon that inward eye
Which is the bliss of solitude[4]:
And then my heart with pleasure fills,
And dances with the daffodils.

[1]**sprightly:** lively
[2]**gay:** happy
[3]**jocund:** cheerful
[4]**solitude:** the state of being alone

GO ON →

8. The rhyme scheme of the first stanza is:
 F. aabbcc
 G. ababcc
 H. abcabc
 J. abbcca

8. _____

9. Personification is the act of assigning human qualities to a nonhuman object or creature. In this poem, Wordsworth personifies daffodils by comparing them to:
 A. poets
 B. clouds
 C. dancers
 D. astronomers

9. _____

10. Upon observing the daffodils, the poet's mood changes from:
 F. bored to interested
 G. concerned to carefree
 H. thoughtless to thoughtful
 J. lonesome to light-hearted

10. _____

11. The daffodils "stretch'd in never-ending line/ Along the margin of a bay." The word *margin* most nearly means:
 A. edge
 B. depth
 C. moisture
 D. curves

11. _____

12. At the end of the third stanza, the narrator still has not realized:
 F. how beautiful the daffodils were
 G. that the beauty of the daffodils cannot last
 H. how this experience would affect him in the future
 J. how this experience would cure his loneliness

12. _____

13. In line 20, the poet refers to "that inward eye" to describe:
 A. how memory operates
 B. a favorite physical feature
 C. what all writers must do
 D. a problem that cannot be fixed

13. _____

14. In line 21, the word "they" refers to:
 F. the stars of the Milky Way
 G. inspirational thoughts
 H. thoughts of loneliness
 J. the daffodils

14. _____

GO ON →

Directions

A myth is a story that has been handed down from generation to generation. Read the myth of Baucis and Philemon and answer the questions that follow.

Baucis and Philemon

From a poem by Ovid

It was said in the ancient Greek world that hospitality was sacred to Zeus, the king of the gods, and it was equally well known that his sidekick, Hermes, loved a practical joke. This explains their involvement in the lives of two mortals, Baucis and Philemon.

Now and then, Zeus would grow bored with the scene in Olympus—drinking nectar and eating ambrosia, watching the Graces dance, listening to Apollo play his lyre—and he would travel to Earth in search of some amusement. One day, Zeus decided to drop by the country of Phrygia to learn who was hospitable and who wasn't. The plan was simple: He and Hermes would disguise themselves as ordinary travelers and at random would knock on people's doors.

The day did not begin well. They visited home after home, humble huts and wealthy abodes, and no one would admit them. And they were treated as rudely as you might imagine: doors slammed in their faces, insulting remarks dismissing them, bolts shoved into place to bar the doors.

At long last, as Zeus and Hermes were about to despair of finding a home inhabited by devout residents, they knocked upon the door of an out-of-the-way hut. Its roof was made of reeds; the tiny hut reeked of poverty. But the door opened wide, and a gentle voice invited them inside.

Zeus and Hermes looked around the hut. Although their heads practically scraped against the low, crumbling roof, the interior of the hut was warm, neat, and comfortable. An old man and his wife introduced themselves—she

GO ON →

was Baucis and he Philemon. Baucis urged her visitors to sit by the fire. Her husband spread a blanket across their legs. They proceeded to prepare a plain meal of stew and olives and roasted eggs.

The two gods came to the table and began to eat. Philemon poured from a mixing bowl two glasses of wine—a thin, diluted, nearly tasteless wine—and he proudly refilled their cups when they were empty. Philemon was so pleased to be of service to his guests that at first he did not notice a strange thing: No matter how often he refilled the cups, the mixing bowl remained full. Then it dawned upon him: These visitors were not men.

He and Baucis bowed before them. They promised to slay and cook a goose they had been saving for a special occasion, but no occasion would be more special than this. They tried to catch the goose, but, with a little help from the gods, the goose eluded capture, and Zeus and Hermes enjoyed the spectacle of their two aged hosts pursuing in vain the elusive creature.

In the end Zeus and Hermes meted out rewards and punishments. They escorted the couple from their home and showed them the surrounding countryside, now covered by a huge lake: Their sinful neighbors had been drowned. Before their tears could dry, Baucis and Philemon noticed that their own hovel had been converted to a magnificent marble temple.

But the best was yet to come. Zeus promised to grant the couple their fondest wish.

The couple lived to a ripe old age, and when the time came for them to pass on, they gazed at each other in amazement, as leaves began to sprout from their arms. Their withered skin turned to dark, firm bark.

Where once they had chased in circles to trap an agile goose, a large tree arose. From one trunk grew two large branches, one linden and one oak. In years to come, visitors to the site would hang wreaths from the branches in tribute to the kind and loving couple.

GO ON →

15. Zeus's and Hermes visit to Phrygia was designed *primarily* to:
- **A.** determine who was virtuous and who was not
- **B.** punish the wicked and reward the good
- **C.** provide some relief from boredom
- **D.** give them a chance to spend a day together

15. _____

16. In Phrygia both the poor and the wealthy:
- **F.** live luxuriously
- **G.** are inhospitable to strangers
- **H.** respect the gods
- **J.** worry about safety and crime

16. _____

17. The description of the home of Baucis and Philemon emphasizes:
- **A.** the difference between its exterior and interior
- **B.** its special location
- **C.** the kindness of its residents
- **D.** the improvements the couple has made

17. _____

18. Zeus and Hermes display their mischievous side when:
- **F.** they provide Baucis and Philemon with a new home
- **G.** they create a lake
- **H.** Baucis and Philemon pursue the goose
- **J.** Baucis and Philemon die

18. _____

19. This myth emphasizes the values of:
- **A.** honesty and self-respect
- **B.** devotion and hospitality
- **C.** kindness and humility
- **D.** pride and competitiveness

19. _____

20. Which of the following best completes this sequence of events:

Zeus and Hermes leave Olympus → Baucis and Philemon admit the gods to their home → _____ → Baucis and Philemon realize the true identity of their guests:

- **F.** the people of Phrygia close their doors to Baucis and Philemon
- **G.** Zeus and Hermes decide to disguise themselves as mortals
- **H.** Baucis and Philemon are granted their dearest wish
- **J.** the mixing bowl remains full with wine

20. _____

GO ON →

Directions

Read the following article on burns and answer the questions that follow.

Don't Play with Matches

I f you're old enough to be reading this, then you've heard that piece of advice a dozen or more times. And it's good advice, too, since every year approximately 500 American children ages fourteen and under die from fire- and burn-related injuries. In 2002, about 92,000 children in that same age group were admitted to hospital emergency rooms for burn injuries. Anyone who has suffered even a minor burn injury knows how painful such an injury can be.

The problem is that the advice is a little simplistic.

Matches create flames, and flames cause a significant number of burn injuries, but other causes produce the same dangers. Scald burn injuries (caused by steam or hot liquids) are especially common among young children. Children are at risk for chemical, electrical, and contact burn injuries, too. Children—especially very young ones—don't necessarily perceive danger; they certainly don't have the ability to respond to a crisis the same way adults do. For example, a young child left in a steaming bath may not be able to adjust the water temperature. Because children's skin is thinner than the skin of adults, they suffer burns more quickly and severely than adults do.

That's why it's essential that grown-ups act like grown-ups. They need to take charge of things, and make these kinds of adjustments:

- You should have a smoke alarm in every level of your home and in every sleeping area. Check the batteries every month, and replace them every year.

GO ON →

■ Did you know that your water heater has a thermostat and that it's easy to adjust? Often thermostats are set to 140 degrees Fahrenheit. Three seconds of exposure to water that hot will leave a child with a third-degree burn. Lowering the thermostat to 120 degrees is a good idea. Install antiscald devices in faucets and shower heads.

■ Never leave a young child in a room by himself. If you have to go to another room—even briefly—take the child with you.

■ Lock up those flammable materials—matches, lighters, gasoline—and keep them away from children.

■ Use some common sense. Don't carry children and hot liquids at the same time. Use the back burners on the stove. Use safety plugs to cover electrical outlets. Don't let your children anywhere near fireworks.

One more suggestion: Encourage politicians to enact burn protection laws. Since 1994, when the U.S. Consumer Product Safety Commission began requiring child-resistant cigarette lighters, the number of fires resulting from children playing with lighters has declined 58%.

---

21. According to the article, the advice "Don't play with matches":

A. needs to be updated

B. doesn't reach a wide enough audience

C. doesn't account for a large number of burn injuries

D. will seem unfamiliar to many of today's readers

21. _____

22. A good title for this article would be:

F. "It's Up to the Firefighters"

G. "Burn Injuries and Young Children"

H. "Education Can Make a Difference"

J. "It's a Question of Common Sense"

22. _____

23. Which piece of evidence would best support the author's point about burn protection laws?

A. Burn protection laws are almost impossible to enforce.

B. Some European countries have even fewer burn protection laws than the United States does.

C. Schools need to take a more active role in teaching fire safety to youngsters.

D. Making products fire-resistant is expensive, so companies won't do it unless they must.

23. _____

GO ON ➔

24. Which of the following does *not* explain why young children are especially vulnerable to burn injuries?

   F. Young children might not recognize a dangerous situation.

   G. The skin of young children burns more easily.

   H. Young children might not know how to treat a burn injury.

   J. Young children might not be able to manipulate their environment.

24. _____

25. The tone of this article can best be described as:

   A. informative and logical

   B. surprised and confused

   C. angry and impatient

   D. gloomy and frustrated

25. _____

GO ON →

Directions

Read this political advertisement, and answer question 26.

Presidential candidates "throw their hats in the ring" when they announce their intention of running for election to the highest office in the land.

Wendy Howard was elected to the City Council in 1982. She quickly earned a reputation as a woman who doesn't mind a good fight. As a councilwoman, she has voted against local tax increases seven times. In 1984 she shaped the legislation that helped turn around our schools. She has long been an outspoken critic of government spending and waste.

Now she wants to be your mayor. District Attorney Raymond Sanchez said, "Wendy Howard loves this city. She'll keep this city safe for us and our children. She deserves your vote."

Wendy Howard wouldn't argue with that.

26. Which of the following is most clearly a statement of opinion?
    F. "Wendy Howard was elected to the City Council in 1982."
    G. "'She'll keep this city safe for us and our children.'"
    H. "As a councilwoman, she has voted against local tax increases seven times."
    J. "Now she wants to be your mayor."

26. _____

GO ON →

PART 2

Listening

Note: You will have 45 minutes to complete Part 2. This does not include the time it takes to listen to the passage twice.

GO ON →

Directions

In this part of the test, you will listen to an essay. The essay appears on page 240 at the end of this chapter. Have a friend or family member read it to you. The essay is entitled "The End of Homework" and was written by a middle school teacher.

You will listen to the essay twice. As you listen, you may want to take notes. You may take notes at any time during the readings. You can use these notes to answer the questions that follow. Use the space below and on the next page for your notes.

Here are some words and definitions you will need to know as you listen to the essay.

■ dodo bird	a bird that is now extinct
■ IMs	instant messages
■ portfolio	collection of work
■ in vogue	popular, fashionable
■ tainted	corrupted, stained
■ avail themselves	use

NOTES

GO ON →

NOTES

GO ON →

27. The author claims that "homework has some pretty stiff competition these days." According to the essay, what are three sources of this competition?

28. The author says that some of the work that students do at home is "tainted." Explain what this sentence means, using information from the essay.

_____

_____

_____

_____

_____

_____

29. The essay says that state tests have affected homework practices. How has this come to pass? Use details from the essay.

_____

_____

_____

_____

_____

_____

GO ON →

PLANNING PAGE

You may PLAN your writing for question 30 here if you wish, but do NOT write your final answer on this page. Your writing on this Planning Page will NOT count toward your final score. Write your final answer beginning on the next page.

GO ON →

30. The author of "The End of Homework" says that there are both good and bad reasons to explain why some teachers are assigning less homework. Explain what you think he means by a good reason. Explain what you think he means by a bad reason. In addition, discuss a reason he hasn't thought of. (Your reason can be either for *or* against assigning less homework.)

In your response, be sure to include:

- what the author thinks is a good reason for teachers assigning less homework
- what the author thinks is a bad reason for teachers assigning less homework
- details from the essay
- what you think would be another reason either for *or* against assigning less homework

✓   **Check your writing for spelling, grammar, and punctuation.**

_____

_____

_____

_____

_____

_____

_____

_____

_____

_____

_____

GO ON →

STOP

PART 3

Reading

 Note: You will have 60 minutes to complete Part 3. You may not go back to Part 1 or Part 2.

GO ON →

Directions

In this part of the test, you will read a poem and an interview. The poem is called "James Jerry Jenkins" and was written by Ron Levine, a middle school administrator. Mr. Levine is the subject of the interview.

James Jerry Jenkins

By Ron Levine

Last week or the one before
Down two doors or maybe more
James Jerry Jenkins opened a store
A giant one with fifty floors

line
5   He doesn't sell shirts, music, or books
You won't find artwork or fishing hooks
But he does have kindness, caring, and compassion
In his store love and laughter are always in fashion

The place stocks the positive aspects of life
10   Don't enter and expect to find sorrow or strife
The workers are super, equipped with wide smiles
And the customers line up for miles and miles

All right, O.K., I see I've been caught
We all know these things—they cannot be bought
15   But imagine if we could pull from his shelves
The traits that we cannot find in ourselves

Maybe all those who do hurting and hating
The faceless terrorists who strap bombs onto babies
Could spend a day shopping, fill up a cart
20   To chase the blackness from out of their hearts

But it's just a dream
Of that I'm aware
You have to be born
With the courage to dare

GO ON →

25   I can't help but be hopeful
                           Don't be angry with me
                         I just wish James Jerry Jenkins
                            Could actually be

---

31. Ron Levine writes, "I just wish James Jerry Jenkins/ Could actually be." Why does he feel this way? Use details from the poem.

_____

_____

_____

_____

_____

_____

GO ON ➜

Directions

AN INTERVIEW WITH RON LEVINE

Ron Levine has spent his entire career working at Great Neck North Middle School on Long Island, first as an English teacher, then as Dean of Students, and now as Assistant Principal. Read this interview, and answer the questions that follow.

Question: Why did you want to become a school administrator? And why middle school?

Ron Levine: While I was a classroom teacher, I became Dean of Students, which provided me the opportunity to see the effect that administrators have on a school. This appealed to me a great deal, and it became a goal of mine to be an administrator. It is the same love of teaching that drives me in this role, and while I do not have the direct effect on children that I had in my classroom, it is my hope that I will have a direct effect on the teachers in all classrooms. Overall, I felt I could take my organizational and leadership skills to the next level and have a greater impact on the educational community. My first experience as a teacher was in the middle school and I found it to be a place ruled by energy and creativity and I wanted to be a part of that. Eleven years later my opinion of middle school and middle level education has not changed; in fact, it has only reinforced my initial impression.

Question: What inspired you to write "James Jerry Jenkins"?

Ron Levine: I had the idea for "James Jerry Jenkins" driving to work one morning, sometime after the Oklahoma City bombing,[1] when Osama bin Laden's name began to surface and play a more prominent role in the evening news. It was the summer before 9/11. I've since taken out of the poem the names of specific individuals. At the time, I was hoping and dreaming of a place, a store, where people purchase the abstract concepts that make the world a better place because the news of the day was weighing me down.

---

[1]In 1995 American terrorists bombed a U.S. government building in Oklahoma City, killing 168 people.

GO ON →

Question: The poem acknowledges that the world has its share of black-hearted people. Since there is no store like the one the poem desires, what can we really do about that situation?

Ron Levine: It all starts with the individual. If we can properly "guide" and "educate" the people we are directly responsible for, beginning with ourselves, I imagine we might arrive at a time when the dark is driven out by light.

By "light" I mean intelligence, knowledge, and nobility. We will never, ever be able to fully drive from the planet the forces that try to drag us down as a whole, but we can severely lessen the impact of these forces if we are well educated and prepared to stand up for what is right.

Question: How do the ideas in a poem like "James Jerry Jenkins" affect the work that you do?

Ron Levine: The position I hold, in a middle school no less, means I have a great responsibility to model the behaviors and ideals within the poem. It serves as a vision for me to help the people in the building, children and adults alike, to focus on what we are here for: to develop young adults who will become positive members of society with a foundation built upon tolerance, appreciation, and understanding.

Question: Do you think the world is getting better or worse?

Ron Levine: Wow. I think that the world is getter better. There seems to be a global awareness about the ills of terrorism, and more countries are beginning to get on board in planning how to combat it. Yet now, in the midst of the situation in Iraq, particularly from an American standpoint, things look bad heading toward worse. So I think this could turn out to be a tough time for our country. How many people look back fondly on the war in Vietnam? And this is what Iraq has become, another Vietnam in too many ways.

Question: What role can poetry—in all its forms—have in the modern world?

Ron Levine: Poetry taps into raw emotion and imagination. In our disposable society, people do not take enough time to sit and reflect upon what drives them, what makes them laugh until it hurts, or what makes them well up with tears. It's go, go, go all the time, and that prohibits us from using

GO ON →

our imagination or stopping to admire a tree caught in a breeze or a child smiling at something that we've lost the ability to smile at over the years. Poetry keeps us human. It is imperative that we never lose sight of that because then we'd be resigned to keeping poetry alive via the Poetry Channel—as if we need more television programming.

32. Ron Levine says, "Poetry keeps us human." What does he mean by this? Use information from the article.

_____

_____

_____

_____

_____

_____

33. Ron Levine is concerned with the responsibilities of adults in middle schools. What are some of these responsibilities? Use details from the article.

GO ON →

PLANNING PAGE

You may PLAN your writing for question 34 here if you wish, but do NOT write your final answer on this page. Your writing on the Planning Page will NOT count toward your final score. Write your final answer on the following pages.

GO ON →

34. People reveal a great deal about themselves through their actions and words. Ron Levine, an educator and a poet, has written a poem, "James Jerry Jenkins," and he has been the subject of an interview. What have you learned about Ron Levine the poet? What have you learned about Ron Levine the educator? How are the two "parts" of Ron Levine similar or different? Use information from BOTH the poem and the interview in your answer.

In your answer be sure to include:

- what you have learned about Ron Levine the poet
- what you have learned about Ron Levine the educator
- a discussion of how the two "parts" of Ron Levine are similar or different
- details from the poem and the interview

✔ **Check your writing for correct spelling, grammar, and punctuation.**

_____

_____

_____

_____

_____

_____

_____

_____

_____

_____

_____

_____

_____

_____

GO ON →

STOP

Answers to Practice Exam Two

ANSWERS TO PART 1: READING COMPREHENSION

1. C	7. B	13. A	19. B	25. A
2. F	8. G	14. J	20. J	26. G
3. B	9. C	15. C	21. C	
4. F	10. J	16. G	22. G	
5. A	11. A	17. A	23. D	
6. J	12. H	18. H	24. H	

The End of Homework

I've been in schools for nearly a half-century, if you count my years as a student and a teacher. I never thought I'd say this, but it looks to me like homework is going the way of the dodo bird.

There are a few reasons for this. Some of them are good; some are bad.

One of the bad ones is that a lot of kids don't do homework—or they do it, but they don't do it well. Some kids are involved in extensive afterschool activities, like sports and clubs and private lessons and religious instruction. By the time they get home and have dinner, they need a little time to unwind, and quality time for homework just doesn't fit into the picture. You can't overlook the fact that homework has some pretty stiff competition these days. It looks to me like kids spend as much time as ever talking to their friends on the phone. Plus now they have 500 channels on their cable TVs and the easy availability of the Internet and IMs, not to mention amazingly lifelike video games. Obviously some of these reasons are better than others, but the result is the same: A significant number of students don't do their homework. For teachers an important reason for assigning homework—maybe the most important reason—is to prepare students for the next day's instruction. It's very frustrating for a teacher to discover that too many students are not ready to participate in the lesson he has planned.

A second reason has to do with a relatively recent change in education: the importance of state tests. Not too long ago, portfolio instruction and assessment were in vogue, and students were evaluated on the work they compiled over a period of time. But with today's assessments, it's all about tasks on demand: What can a student do on test days? The result is that classroom time is being used differently. Students are using class time to complete tasks similar to those they'll encounter on tests. In social studies, for example, they'll go to the library and read real historical documents and write DBQs. In English students will listen to a speaker and learn how to take notes. In other words, because of state tests, schoolwork is much less dependent upon what students do outside the class.

Besides, some of that out-of-class work is tainted. Students, especially those who come from affluent families, may avail themselves of questionable resources: They're getting help from parents, siblings, tutors, and internet sources, and in many cases there's a very thin line between "helping" and "cheating." In any case, on state tests, students will not have these sources at their disposal.

There are still some reasons to assign homework. Certainly homework can be used as a review exercise, as a way of strengthening newly acquired skills. Also, homework can be used to develop good lifelong habits; outside reading assignments try to satisfy this goal. Finally, there's one more reason: Parents expect their children to have some homework, and they can be very irritable when they don't.

---

30. The author of "The End of Homework" says that there are both good and bad reasons to explain why some teachers are assigning less homework. Explain what you think he means by a good reason. Explain what you think he means by a bad reason. In addition, discuss a reason he hasn't thought of. (Your reason can be either for *or* against assigning less homework.)

In your response, be sure to include:

- what the author thinks is a good reason for teachers assigning less homework
- what the author thinks is a bad reason for teachers assigning less homework

- details from the essay
- what you think would be another reason either for *or* against assigning less homework

 Check your writing for spelling, grammar, and punctuation.

Can anyone really imagine a time when students no longer receive homework assignments? It sounds too good to be true, right? Well, one experienced middle school teacher thinks that day is right around the corner. However, although some of the causes of this possible event are positive, others are negative.

One positive cause is the new battery of state tests. These tests place a priority on on-demand tasks, the kinds of tasks that students actually have to perform on the assessments. So, instead of going home to complete boring homework assignments (possibly with the questionable help of a tutor or Sparks Notes), students spend classtime on valuable activities. An example is the DBQs that students write in social studies. Students would read actual historical documents and answer questions based on these. This is clearly a better use of a student's time and effort.

One not-so-good reason is the fact that some students just don't bother to complete assignments. Instead of setting aside the time to do homework, some students spend hour after hour talking on the phone, watching television, playing video games, or sending instant messages on their personal computers. Teachers base their lessons on the idea that students will be prepared, but when too many are unprepared, those plans have to go out the window.

The author of this essay is in a tricky situation, but he should not give up on homework altogether. You'd probably have a hard time finding too many kids who would admit to enjoying homework, but a lot of kids recognize that homework is important. It gives students a chance to review material taught in class, and it allows students to look ahead to the next day's instruction. Finally, completing homework assignments is a productive use of a person's time. After all, how many hours of TV can a kid watch, anyway?

ANSWER TO PART 3: READING

34. People reveal a great deal about themselves through their actions and words. Ron Levine, an educator and a poet, has written a poem, "James Jerry Jenkins," and he has been the subject of an interview. What have you learned about Ron Levine, the poet? What have you learned about Ron Levine, the educator? How are the two "parts" of Ron Levine similar or different? Use information from BOTH the poem and the interview in your answer.

In your answer be sure to include:

■ what you have learned about Ron Levine, the poet
■ what you have learned about Ron Levine, the educator
■ a discussion of how the two "parts" of Ron Levine are similar or different
■ details from the poem and the interview

 Check your writing for correct spelling, grammar, and punctuation.

The words that people say and the actions they perform tell a lot about who they are. This is certainly true of Ron Levine, a school administrator on Long Island and the author of "James Jerry Jenkins," a poem.

Ron Levine's poem was inspired by the Oklahoma City bombing and other acts of terrorism. Events of this kind could affect a person powerfully, and they had just that effect on Ron Levine the poet. In his interview, he complains about the "go-go-go" lifestyle that "prohibits us from using our imagination." Yet in his poem he has imagined a store that sells the kind of human qualities that would improve the world—qualities that would "chase the blackness" from the hearts of those who would do evil. Even though he admits that no such store really exists, he believes that regular people, such as school administrators, can make a difference.

As an educator, Ron Levine seems determined to make a difference. In his interview he admits that teachers exert the most direct influence in schools, but he also has come to understand that administrators can have an impact on an entire educational community. That impact, it seems, is mostly about inspiring individuals. Ron Levine talks about the power of "intelligence, knowledge, and nobility." These are qualities that administrators can model for teachers and that teachers can instill in students. To Ron Levine, this seems like the best work schools can accomplish if they use their energy and creativity well. If schools can accomplish these goals, they can make a real difference in the world.

Ron Levine the poet and Ron Levine the educator are very much the same person. Both believe deeply in the power of dreams, imagination, hope, and creativity. These qualities can be seen in James Jerry Jenkins's imaginary store and in Ron Levine's idealistic belief in the potential of schools. But the poem and the interview also reveal Ron Levine's concerns about where the world seems to be headed. In both cases, there's a real gap between what is real and what can be imagined.